WILLIAM ROBERTSON SMITH

Anthropology's Ancestors

Edited by Aleksandar Bošković, University of Belgrade; Institute of Archaeology, Belgrade; Max Planck Institute for Social Anthropology, Halle/Saale

As anthropology developed across geographical, historical, and social boundaries, it was always influenced by works of exceptional scholars who pushed research topics in new and original directions and who can be regarded as important ancestors of the discipline. The aim of this series is to offer introductions to these major figures, whose works constitute landmarks and are essential reading for students of anthropology, but who are also of interest for scholars in the humanities and social sciences more generally. In doing so, it offers important insights into some of the basic questions facing humanity.

Volume 2
William Robertson Smith
Aleksandar Bošković

Volume 1
Margaret Mead
Paul Shankman

WILLIAM ROBERTSON
SMITH

• • •

Aleksandar Bošković

berghahn
NEW YORK • OXFORD
www.berghahnbooks.com

First published in 2021 by
Berghahn Books
www.berghahnbooks.com

Library of Congress Cataloging-in-Publication Data

A C.I.P. cataloging record is available from the Library of Congress

Library of Congress Cataloging in Publication Control Number:
2021028081

British Library Cataloguing in Publication Data

A catalogue record for this book is available from the British Library

ISBN 978-1-80073-157-8 hardback
ISBN 978-1-80073-158-5 paperback
ISBN 978-1-80073-159-2 ebook

CONTENTS

● ● ●

FIGURES

• • •

PREFACE

●　●　●

During my postgraduate studies at Tulane University in New Orleans, I decided to focus on William Robertson Smith's study of myth and ritual. This decision (and a significant change in my academic plans at the time, as I came to Tulane to study ancient Mayas) was partly the result of a chance visit to the library of the Pittsburgh Theological Seminary in 1992. This happened during a visit to my friends, Svetlana and Milan Vukomanović. (Milan defended his PhD in Religious Studies at the University of Pittsburgh, and was teaching there, until 1995.) The library had different editions of Smith's books, so I was able to see revisions that he made and the extent to which he was in dialogue with the leading scholars of his time. This library also had different editions of *Encyclopædia Britannica*. Therefore, I was able to compare these different editions and could realize the extent to which this monument of scholarship was transformed under Smith's editorship. All of this helped me appreciate the extent of his knowledge and influence, as well as the importance of his work. In April 1993, I defended my MA thesis, supervised by Professor Munro S. Edmonson (1924–2002). As I continued with my doctoral studies in Scotland, in early April 1994 I attended the William Robertson Smith Congress in Aberdeen. Some of Smith's ideas on myth and ritual were important parts of the courses on myth (both undergraduate and graduate) that I taught at the University of Brasília (Brazil) in 1999 and 2000, as well as in the courses on religion and ritual at the University of the Witwatersrand in Johannesburg (South Africa) in 2002. In the meantime, I published a thoroughly revised version of my MA thesis in one of the leading Brazilian anthropology journals, *Anuário Antropológico* (Bošković 2002). Some of my colleagues from Brasília, as well as the essay's readers, provided important insights that helped this publication take its final form. However, although Smith's work remained an important part of my subsequent teaching, both in courses on the history of anthropology and in the ones dealing with myth and religion, I did not anticipate that I would return to focus exclusively on him.

The idea of going back to Smith, as well as looking further into his general influence on various scholars referred to as "myth-ritualists," was in 2015 first suggested by my friend and esteemed colleague, Professor Israel Knohl from the Department of the Bible, Hebrew University in Jerusalem, while we were both attending a conference in Mostar (Bosnia and Herzegovina). I am very grateful to him and to Professor Michael Segal, dean of the Faculty of Humanities at the time, for the opportunity, in Jerusalem on 7 January 2016, to present my initial research about the relationship between William Robertson Smith and the myth-ritualists in the Department of the Bible seminar. As I continued working on this subject, a different version of that paper was presented in the same year at the Masaryk University, Brno, Czech Republic, on 28 May. Revised versions (in Serbo-Croatian) were also presented in the symposium following the publication of the *Dictionary of Deities and Mythic Personalities of the World* (published in Serbo-Croatian), which took place at the Institute of Social Sciences in Belgrade, Serbia, on 9 June (Bošković, Vukomanović, and Jovanović 2015), and later in the same year (2016) at the Franciscan Theological Faculty in Sarajevo, Bosnia and Herzegovina, on 30 November. For the invitation to the Franciscan Theological Faculty, and hospitality provided there, I am most grateful to Professor Mile Babić. In 2017, I presented my research at the Center for Anthropological and Spatial Studies, Slovenian Academy of Sciences and Arts in Ljubljana, Slovenia, on 30 January (for which I very much appreciate the invitation of Professor Borut Telban and the assistance and friendship of Professor Maja Petrović Šteger). Following the kind invitation of Dr. David Shankland, director of the Royal Anthropological Institute (RAI), the final version (which forms an important part of the present book) was presented at the RAI's research seminar in London on 31 May 2017. I benefitted greatly from the discussions, comments, and questions that followed these presentations and seminars. As I was preparing a final version for the RAI seminar, Dr. Marion Berghahn came up with an idea of a new series on Anthropology's Ancestors for Berghahn Books, and this manuscript came as a result of that project.

ACKNOWLEDGMENTS

* * *

During the work on this manuscript, I was very fortunate to get in touch with Mrs. Astrid Hess, owner of the William Robertson Smith website and great-granddaughter of Smith's sister, Alice Thiele Smith (1858–1943). She kindly provided me with important additional information (including copies of Smith's letters from the journey to Sicily and Egypt, Leask's book, and some correspondence referred to in it) and made available to me some of her family photos, as well as Gordon K. Booth's PhD thesis. Her invaluable assistance provided me with a unique insight into the life of a Scottish family in the mid-nineteenth century.

In the course of doing the finishing touches on the present text, between February and April 2018, I was able to spend six weeks at the University of Aberdeen, thanks to the kind invitation and hospitality of a friend and colleague who at that time worked in the School of Education, Dr. Salma Siddique. While in Aberdeen (as well as afterward), I also benefited from the help and insights of Professor Robert Segal, today probably the most knowledgeable person on myth, ritual, and comparative perspective in the study of myths. He also offered me help with many materials (including references to particular archives) that I would normally need months to find. Professor Segal wrote extensively about Smith, including the foreword to the 2002 edition of the *Lectures on the Religion of the Semites*, which makes him a scholar uniquely qualified in this area. Professor Raquel Weiss from the Universidade Federal de Rio Grande de Sul in Brazil helped me by pointing out several publications that clarify Durkheim's appreciation of Smith's work. Last but not least, my friend and former colleague from the University of Brasília, Mariza G. S. Peirano, influenced my interest in the "anthropology of anthropology" some two decades ago, and I am forever grateful for that.

While I am both honored and humbled to have associated with so many fantastic people and brilliant scholars during my work on this book, none of them is responsible for any potential errors or omissions.

Finally, I should note that a part of the work on this book was made available through the funding provided by the Ministry of Science, Education and Technology of the Republic of Serbia, as part of the project III 47010, which I directed between January 2011 and April 2018. My initial trip to the William Robertson Smith Congress in 1994 was supported by a grant from the University of St. Andrews Travel Fund. The manuscript was completed while I was a research fellow at the Institute for Advanced Studies in Lyon (Collegium de Lyon, Institut d'études avancées) in 2019.

NOTES ON TEXT

Some of the texts quoted use terms that are now considered obsolete or offensive, such as "savage," "tribe," etc. Additionally, Smith and his contemporaries did not use gender-neutral language. The quotations are from the original texts, so the spelling varies, depending on the author and the country of publication (United Kingdom or United States). All the names of places in Arabic are quoted as they appear in the original books or articles.

INTRODUCTION

• • •

The main aim of this book is to present the life and career of one of anthropology's most important ancestors, William Robertson Smith (1846–1894), in the context of the history of anthropology and the development of different anthropological concepts. Following his early interest in the sacrifice of animals and plants, totemism, and the study of kinship and marriage in Early Arabia, Smith was one of the scholars who profoundly influenced the development and establishment of anthropology as an academic discipline in the late nineteenth century. He drew from the theories of kinship at the time, while they were being established and formulated, and insisted on the importance of totemism. His concept of the relationship between myth and ritual influenced generations of scholars, both in anthropology and sociology, and in the so-called "myth and ritual school." That is why his influence on the studies of the relationship between myth and ritual will take a significant part of the present book—especially since the connections between him and especially Scandinavian "myth-ritualists" have so far been ignored.

Although respected and studied, especially since the 1990s,[1] Smith has a somewhat paradoxical position in the history of social and cultural anthropology.[2] Anthropologists educated in the twentieth century admire him, but many contemporary scholars are not quite sure what to make of him. This is the result of the lack of understanding of the extent of his influence on scholars such as Sir James George Frazer (1854–1941)—a close friend who dedicated the first edition of *The Golden Bough* to Smith,[3] Émile Durkheim (1858–1917), Marcel Mauss (1872–1950), Bronislaw

Malinowski (1884–1942), Sir E. E. Evans-Pritchard (1902–1973),[4] and their followers.[5] As a matter of fact, Durkheim was very clear in acknowledging his debt to Smith in his *Elementary Forms of Religious Life*—and he even went as far as to claim that he changed the way in which he saw religion, after having read Smith's *Lectures* in 1895 (Maryanski 2014: 354; Isambert 1976: 41). According to a historian of anthropology and archaeology, Durkheim was decisively influenced by Smith in developing "the idea that periodic forms of ceremony were vital in sustaining the individual's commitment to the community" (Gosden 1999: 77). Also very important is Smith's influence on the whole development of the distinction between the *sacred* and the *profane* among the whole generation of French scholars (as claimed by Borgeaud 1994: 594). Unsurprisingly, given his own appreciation by (as well as his influence on) Durkheim, Smith's work was also very highly regarded by one of the most important social anthropologists of the twentieth century, A. R. Radcliffe-Brown (1881–1955). This is obvious from the following observation reprinted in a collection of essays published several years after Radcliffe-Brown died: "Important contributions to social anthropology were made by historians such as Fustel de Coulanges, Henry Maine and Robertson Smith. The last named writer is particularly important as the pioneer in the sociological study of religion in his work on early Semitic religion" (Radcliffe-Brown 1958: 161). Finally, and for quite some time, there have been a number of scholars who point to the extent to which the founding father of psychoanalysis, Sigmund Freud (1856–1939), was also influenced by some of Smith's ideas about totem and sacrifice (Rieff 1954: 529; Jones 1980: 512; Segal 2000: 261; Booth 2002)—especially in the fourth part of his seminal work, *Totem and Taboo* (chapter titled "The Return of Totemism in Childhood").[6]

After Radcliffe-Brown, another notable twentieth-century anthropologist who fully appreciated the importance and relevance of Smith's work was Dame Mary Douglas (1921–2007). In her classic work *Purity and Danger* (1966: 24, quoted by Sharpe 1986: 81), she compared Smith's ideas to the ones of the founder of modern anthropology, Sir Edward Burnett Tylor

(1832–1917): "Whereas Tylor was interested in what quaint relics can tell us of the past, Robertson Smith was interested in the common elements in modern and primitive experience. Tylor founded folk-lore [*sic*]: Robertson Smith founded social anthropology."[7] Perhaps she gave Smith a little bit more credit than he deserves (the claim that he "founded social anthropology" seems a bit too generous), but it certainly points to the extent of his influence. For example, Malinowski was very much impressed by his insistence on observing what people actually do (as opposed to what they believe in—as noted by his biographer Michael Young [2004: 235]).[8] In the last couple of decades, and especially following the publication of the papers delivered at the William Robertson Smith Congress in April 1994 (Johnstone 1995), there has been quite a bit of renewed interest in Smith's work and legacy. For example, in Tim Ingold's inaugural lecture, in 2003, as the Chair in Social Anthropology was being re-established at the University of Aberdeen, he referred to Smith as "a giant of scholarship" (2004: 184). At the same time, Ingold also emphasized on Smith's arguments in opposition to what the founder of social anthropology, Tylor, claimed about "primitive beliefs" (Ingold 2004: 186–187). Unfortunately, Smith is absent from the otherwise quite extensive *Biographical Dictionary of Social and Cultural Anthropology* (Amit 2004), but it seems that an interest in his work has intensified in the last decade. More recently, the leading historian of contemporary social anthropology, Adam Kuper, also pointed to Smith's importance for the development of the emerging scholarly discipline and its relationship to the study of the Bible (2016: 7–10).

When it comes to the specific biographical details about Smith's life, very little can be added to the classic early texts, such as Black and Chrystal's detailed biography (1912a), or the abridged version as presented by Bryce (1903). These key texts are referred to in all the subsequent dictionaries, encyclopedias, etc.—whenever Smith's name is mentioned. His sister, Alice Thiele Smith, the only child from the family who married and had her own children, left a beautifully written memoir about growing up in mid-nineteenth-century Aberdeenshire (Thiele

Smith 2004). For readers interested in more specific aspects of Smith's theological work, Maier (2009) offers impressive details of his correspondence with Wellhausen, and he also presents a detailed account of Smith's communication with (and influences by) contemporary German scholars in the second half of the nineteenth century (2009: 86ff.). I should also mention that a special issue of the *Journal of Scottish Thought* was dedicated to him and published in 2008. Smith's papers and correspondence are available in the archives at the Cambridge University Library, Christ's College at Cambridge, University of Aberdeen, and University College London. As the technology develops, and the need to preserve the legacy of past scholarship is considered increasingly important; in recent years, many of his books have been made available in digital format—making his ideas much more accessible than they were several decades ago. This is to a great extent due to the efforts of his family, as can be seen on the website https://william-robertson-smith.net/en/.

However, the main reason for writing this book is the reconsideration and proper evaluation of Smith as one of the most important ancestors of anthropology, placing him firmly within the history of our discipline. This is not another biography of William Robertson Smith—the biographies by Black and Chrystal and by Maier are very good. This book is more like a journey through anthropology and related disciplines with Smith as the guide. The main aim of this book is to demonstrate specific examples of his influence on the development and establishment of some key concepts of social anthropology, such as totemism. I am interested in the reception of different concepts, as well as the ways they have been reinterpreted. As already mentioned above, and as will become obvious in the following pages, I find especially significant the anthropological study of myth, and it is easy to see the general influence that Smith's ideas had on some very important anthropologists, as well as on different representatives of the myth and ritual school. Although the extent of Smith's importance has already been recognized from the early twentieth century, there was still an impressive omission in studying the extent to which members of the so-called "Uppsala school" (primarily

Scandinavian scholars) were themselves influenced by his views on myth and ritual, and later developed further some of Smith's ideas—not only about the relationship between myth and ritual, but also his concept of the "comparative study of religion."[9] There are also some important (mis)conceptions about anthropology's ancestors (Smith included), and I intend to show how some twentieth-century critical assessments of his work (like the one on "Smith the Orientalist") were not based on facts, but on very particular readings, intentionally taken out of context.

In the first part of this book, I will present a brief overview of Smith's life—focusing on his relationship with some other notable ancestors of anthropology. At the same time, it should be stressed that Smith saw himself not only as a theologian, but also (and, in my view, primarily) as a scientist who was trying to *rationally* explain behavior and beliefs of the peoples that he studied, using the most advanced scientific theories of his time. Smith's whole career coincides with the industrial revolution and the epoch of great scientific advances and great discoveries, which led nineteenth-century scholars to believe that everything can be explained. His first teaching experience was also in the area of natural sciences. The fact is, after all, that Smith originally won a bursary for mathematics, and immediately afterward studied natural sciences. This aspect of his work (his so-called "formative years") was explored in great detail in Gordon K. Booth's admirable PhD thesis, defended at the University of Aberdeen (1999). In his work, Booth clearly demonstrates the extent to which Smith's ideas should be considered in the context of the social, cultural, and historical conditions of the time, the mid-nineteenth-century Scottish cultural and academic milieu, and Smith's own character (he was always eager to enter into a vigorous debate, especially when he was younger—and sometimes even on behalf of his teachers or mentors), as well as in light of the specific individuals with whom he worked and socialized. All of these elements influenced his views and ideas—as well as their immediate reception by his peers or critics.

I will then turn to his fieldwork experience—against the commonly held (and factually wrong) view that Smith (as well as some of his more famous contemporaries, like Tylor) was an "armchair anthropologist"—focusing on his ethnographic accounts from several trips to Egypt and the Arabian peninsula, primarily through his notes and observations published in the journals and magazines of his time. This fieldwork experience makes Smith a little bit unusual and at the same time quite original for the time when he lived and worked (when it was believed that firsthand field observations were mostly reserved for adventurers, travelers, or missionaries)—but very modern and contemporary in other aspects. As far as I know, letters from Smith's travel to Sicily and Egypt have never been reprinted since their original publication in the *Scotsman*.

I will then proceed with a brief discussion of his view on myth and ritual, and follow it by tracing how his idea of their relationship developed in anthropology well into 1970s and 1980s. After all, "Smith remains the pioneering myth-ritualist because he was the first to propose that the earliest myths arose in connection with rituals" (Segal 1998: 3). In order to fully grasp the significance of his work, it is also important to provide a brief outline of the ways in which some other scholars who have approached the study of myth wrote about it and explained it before the late nineteenth century.

I will also point to some important works of several Scandinavian scholars (plus one British American), who further developed some of Smith's key ideas (especially from his studies of the Old Testament, as well as his methodology of Biblical criticism) in the first half of the twentieth century. Even though Smith was not always referred to, and neither was he properly referenced, his work and his ideas were obviously present in their work. It will become obvious that the extent of Smith's influence has been vastly underappreciated, and I hope to be able to demonstrate this influence not only in the studies of religious (and spiritual) aspects of human life, but also in our understanding of the social aspects—especially when it comes to the uses of myth and ritual in historical and political contexts.

In the final part of this book, I will deal with some more sociological aspects of Smith's work—primarily when it comes to the relationship that people *as members of societies* have with the political (as well as social, cultural, etc.) institutions of their societies—this means people as members of "nations," different ethnic groups, or participants in "national cultures." In writing about these connections, Smith was again well ahead of his time, and his work preceded some important contemporary anthropologists interested in understanding the "myths of the state" (Goody 1968; Kapferer 1988; Bošković 2013).

NOTES

1. Among the critical studies of his work, see, e.g., Brown 1964; Beidelman 1974a; Nelson 1969, 1973; and Bailey 1970. An excellent critique of Smith's views on religion was offered by Warburg (1989).

2. This is the case primarily in the American anthropological tradition. Actually, he is the only nineteenth-century anthropologist who is very highly regarded among British social anthropologists (Sharpe 1986: 81). Except for Beidelman, all the scholars who have been mentioned in the first note are not anthropologists.

3. Although by 1900, when the second edition of *The Golden Bough* was published, he had changed his mind, and explicitly rejected the observations (by the leading French scholars of religion and ritual of that time, Mauss and Hubert) that he had been influenced by Smith (Ackerman 2008: 73).

   On the other hand, his biographer claims that Frazer was decisively influenced by meeting "an even more brilliant jewel in Scotland's intellectual crown, the theologian and historian of Semitic religion William Robertson Smith" (Ackerman 2015: 2).

4. See also Beidelman 1974b: 558. Thomas Beidelman (1974b: 562) also refers to Evans-Pritchard's statement (although, as he noted, not put in print) that the concept of segmentary societies derived from Smith's *Kinship and Marriage in Early Arabia*, published in 1885, as well as from Henry Maine's *Ancient Law*, published in 1861.

5. With the exception of important studies by Jones (1984) and Ackerman (1973, 1991). In another book, Jones (2005: 3) claims that matters are more complicated, and that Durkheim actually did not refer to Smith, but to Frazer instead, in the years following his "discovery" of Smith's method, after 1895. For me, this comes down to whether one would believe Durkheim (as I do), or Jones.

6. On the other hand, and without getting into a detailed discussion of this topic here, it could also be argued that Freud (2001: 119–122) actually refers to Smith's works through the lens of J. G. Frazer, who had radically different views about the place and the role of totems in society. Some aspects that Freud (2001: 154) mentions ("primal horde," "death of the father," sibling rivalry) actually come from other authors (Darwin, Atkinson, and other psychoanalysts such as Ferenczi and Rank), and Smith's contribution to his book ("totem meal") occupies a relatively minor place.

   Freud was very methodical in his writing, and always sought to include the most relevant and the most up to date ethnographic accounts to illustrate his theories.

7. Sharpe immediately notes that "Tylor, of course, did not found folklore." In all fairness to Tylor, he himself refers to the new discipline that he was writing about as *ethnography* (Tylor 1871, vol. 1: 1). Of course, this is the time period (the second half of the nineteenth century) when terms such as "anthropology," "ethnology," and "ethnography" were all used interchangeably—and sometimes even by the same scholars in the same texts (Bošković 2010).

8. This is the point I will return to when discussing his idea of the primacy of ritual over myth.

9. The only exception is Segal's work, especially the anthology that he edited (1998). It is somewhat strange that this excellent volume has been out of print for quite some time. That might be at least in part because contemporary anthropologists (and social scientists in general) tend to stay away from reading texts about myths and religion—unlike their colleagues who wrote about the same topics before World War II.

CHAPTER 1

THE LIFE OF
WILLIAM ROBERTSON SMITH

● ● ●

There was nothing that he undertook of which he did not immediately become a master. His mind seemed to be the most perfect intellectual machine ever designed by the almighty for the equipment of a mortal. It absorbed, coordinated, generalized, transmuted and recreated knowledge with incredible swiftness, and every process was informed with the exactitude and candour of the mathematician.

—Donald Carswell, *Brother Scots*

William Robertson Smith was born on 8 November 1846, at the New Farm in the valley of Don, parish of Keig, Aberdeenshire, Scotland,[1] the second of eleven children (and the oldest son) of William Pirie Smith (1811–1890) and Jane Robertson (1824–1900). The place where he was born was described by one of his contemporaries as "a sweet and peaceful district, with a tranquil, sylvan beauty, the silver stream winding through it and the hills bending down upon it" (Salmond 1894: 357). His mother was the daughter of William Robertson, head of the West End Academy, Aberdeen—where his father was a teacher. Smith had four brothers (but one died immediately after birth) and six sisters. Jane Robertson "was a woman of great force of character, who retained till her death, at seventy-six years of age [in 1900], the full exercise of her keen intelligence" (Bryce 1903: 312). His father was a minister in the parish's Free Church of Scotland, which came into existence after the 1843 split in the Church of Scotland. A man of extraordinary erudition, Pirie Smith taught his children at home until it was time for them to attend the university. Among other things, he taught them Latin, Greek, mathematics, and "rational conversation." Robertson Smith's classmate was his fifteen-months-younger brother George—and the main goal of education was to prepare them for entrance to the University of Aberdeen. According to his biographers, Black and Chrystal (1912a: 11–12), Smith learned the Hebrew alphabet and was able to read Hebrew words before he was six.

After winning a prestigious Ferguson scholarship, Smith entered the University of Aberdeen in 1861 to study mathematics,[2] and graduated in 1865 with a Master of Arts degree and the Town Council Medal, as the best student of that year. But Smith and his brother were not liked by everyone. In his anecdotal history of the University of Aberdeen, W. Keith Leask (1917: 216) mentions "the Smith legend":

> No two men have worked such mischief in the Arts Faculty as did the two brothers from Keig in 1861–65. Were they not held up as demigods to succeeding Classes? "By our own spirits are we deified," and the professoriate with the whole North created, fostered, begot, and adulated with the maddest of hallelujahs this unfortunate type.

Leask (1917: 216–217) paints an unflattering portrait of two young men who apparently did not show any respect for authority—"The poor white-faced boys from Keig used to be seen running out at night, hand in hand, for a breath of fresh air!"— but who were always encouraged and praised by their parents, especially their mother. However, as Booth (1999: ch. 3) explains in great detail in his thesis, these attacks on Smith and his family should be put in context of some contemporary debates of the time, as well as Smith's youthful desire to enter into vigorous discussions with his contemporaries (sometimes local celebrities or university professors) that he perceived as hostile to (or too critical of) his teachers and intellectual mentors.

Figure 1.1. Jane Robertson and William Pirie Smith on their wedding day. Family photos, courtesy of Astrid Hess. Reprinted with permission.

Figure 1.2. William Robertson Smith, 1854. Family photos, courtesy of Astrid Hess. Reprinted with permission.

In 1866, Smith entered New College in Edinburgh, where he studied under A. B. Davidson (1831–1902), professor of Hebrew and Old Testament exegesis, who had a profound influence on him and probably inspired his interest in Semitic studies. However, at the time Smith was also very much interested in physics and "natural philosophy," and got his first teaching experience as assistant to P. G. Tait (1831–1901), professor and head of the natural philosophy department at the University of Edinburgh (and also one of the most influential British scientists in the second half of the nineteenth century), in 1868/1869. It seems that

Figure 1.3. Mary Jane, Isabella, George, and William Robertson Smith in Aberdeen, 1860. Family photos, courtesy of Astrid Hess. Reprinted with permission.

at this time Smith still had not made a final decision on whether
he would devote his career to Biblical studies, the church and religion, or to natural philosophy (or physics, as it would be called
today)—as he seemed equally capable in all of these disciplines.

It was also remarkable that he assisted Tait with what were
known as the "Ladies Classes." Women in Edinburgh had
newly been permitted to attend separate lectures in certain subjects at university level and to sit exams, but not
to graduate. In one report Robertson Smith stated that
the best female students in the Natural Philosophy class
undoubtedly reached a level of achievement comparable
with that of the most able male students, although he felt
that the women often hesitated to insist on their point of
view even if they recognised a counter-argument as *non-
sense*. (Hess, n.d., "Biography: Childhood, First Lessons
and Study)

At the same time (between 1867 and 1869), Smith made several trips to Germany (to Bonn, Heidelberg, and Göttingen),
where he continued his studies of physics and mathematics, but
also became acquainted with the works of the Old Testament
scholars associated with "higher criticism" (primarily Albrecht
Ritschl [1822–1889] and Abraham Kuenen [1828–1891]).[3] These
scholars made a lasting impression on him (Meier 2009). In 1871,
he was elected Fellow of the Royal Society of Edinburgh, after
being nominated by P. G. Tait.

Smith spent the summer of 1872 in Göttingen, learning Arabic
with the leading Asian (then-called Oriental) studies scholar at
the time, Paul de Lagarde (1827–1891), and also meeting Julius
Wellhausen (1844–1918),[4] who would become a lifelong friend.
John Sutherland Black (1846–1923), his fellow student at New
College (actually one year ahead of Smith), also became a friend
for life, occasional travel companion, and—much later—his most
important and most reliable biographer. While in Edinburgh,
Smith also met John Ferguson McLennan (1827–1881), lawyer
and ethnologist from Inverness, who would influence him to

develop an interest in studying kinship, marriage patterns, and totemism—eventually leading to studies that would later shape the emerging discipline of social anthropology. McLennan published his *Primitive Marriage* in 1865. This was a book in which he developed a social evolutionist view of kinship, and argued that some forms of matrilineality were a necessary evolutionary stage in the development of all human societies.[5] He was also the first nineteenth-century scholar who wrote about totemism, first in a brief encyclopedia article in 1868, and a little bit later in much more detail in the *Fortnightly Review* in 1869/1870, decisively influencing Smith's interest in the subject (and Smith later influenced Frazer's interest in the same topic).[6] McLennan believed that totems were original gods, and that they arose at the same time the patrilineal groups were formed.

With the support of Davidson, Smith was in 1870 elected to the Chair of Oriental Languages and Old Testament exegesis of the Free Church College at Aberdeen. At the same time, he was also ordained a minister. Smith's inaugural lecture, "What History Teaches Us to Look for in the Bible," published immediately after he delivered it, already pointed to the direction of his interest, as well as to the influences from continental Europe. Smith taught there until 1876, when a controversy surrounding several of his articles for the ninth edition of the *Encyclopædia Britannica* (especially the entry "Bible," published in the third volume in December 1875)[7] forced him to withdraw from teaching. In this important *Encyclopædia* article, Smith (1875: 636) wrote, "It is plain, however, that the whole work is not the uniform production of one pen, but that in some way a variety of records of different ages and styles have been combined to form a single narrative." For the predominantly conservative members of the Church, especially contentious was Smith's (1875: 637–638) development (and elucidation) of a distinction between "priestly" and "prophetic" narratives. He was accused of heresy and tried, but successfully defended himself, so the formal charges had to be dropped.[8] However, the controversy was renewed after the publication of his article "Animal Worship and Animal Tribes among the Arabs and in the Old Testament" in the *Journal of Philology* in June 1880, after which he was forced to resign from teaching. Despite this resignation, W. R. Smith remained a minister in the Free Church of Scotland (for a wider context of the heresy trial, see also Livingstone 2015). As put by a more contemporary observer, in another biographical sketch of Smith's life,

> The Bible was regarded by the Free Church of Scotland as "the supreme rule of faith and life," and so anything that might seem to undermine its authority was bound to arouse opposition. An investigation by the college committee of the Free Church found that Smith's opinions as expressed in the article "Bible" were hardly compatible with his position as a teacher of candidates for the ministry of the church, but provided insufficient grounds to support a process for heresy. Smith maintained that he accepted that the Bible was the one sufficient and authoritative record of divine revelation, and that his critical views were the fruit of studies carried out under the guidance of his teachers at New College, Edinburgh. He therefore demanded that he be given a formal trial by libel (indictment) for his alleged heresies and errors. In the subsequent protracted proceedings in the various church courts Smith, by sheer dialectical skill, was able to beat back the attack on all points except the authorship and purpose of Deuteronomy. The libel proceedings were eventually terminated, but a vote of no confidence in Smith was passed by the general assembly of 1881 and was followed by his summary removal from his chair. (Sefton 2004)

The publicity surrounding the trial brought him immense support, not only from leading European scholars such as Kuenen and Wellhausen, but also from the younger clergy and many of his countrymen. As a consequence of his sudden fame, he was invited to give a series of lectures in Edinburgh and Glasgow. These lectures were a huge success, very popular with the public, and they were published in 1881 as *The Old Testament in the Jewish*

Figure 1.4. A sketch depicting Smith as a boy trying to avoid being devoured by crocodiles. An impression of the heresy trial, probably drawn by Smith himself. Copy of the original drawing, provided by Astrid Hess. Reprinted with permission.

Church. Another series of lectures was given the following winter, and they were published in 1882 as *The Prophets of Israel and Their Place in History to the Close of the Eighth Century B.C.*

Alice MacDonell, daughter of one of his friends, remembers Smith from this period as "the most dogmatic." She wrote that "the heresy hunt which evicted him from Chair as Professor of Hebrew in the Free Church College of Aberdeen had turned him into a 'bonny fetcher.'" According to her, Cambridge greeted him "with open arms," but he still loved the Church. "He used to stay he had gained *one* benefit from his bitter experience in Aberdeen—he could now discard his clerical tie and revel in flaming 'Liberty scarves'" (MacDonell 1933: 35). Some of his important lifelong friendships were formed in this period, including the one with a fellow Aberdonian, artist Sir George Reid (1841–1913). Reid was responsible for some of the most important and well-known portraits of Smith, but also of some members of his family.

In 1881, the year he lost his position in Aberdeen, Smith became the assistant editor and then, in 1883—following the illness of the editor, Professor Thomas Spencer Baynes (1823–1887)—editor-in-chief of the ninth edition of the *Encyclopædia Britannica*, a post that he held until the completion of this project in 1889. The ninth edition was essential in setting the highest standards of the *Encyclopædia Britannica* for the decades to come, and it brought together an unprecedented number of highly qualified scholars, partly due to the immense breadth of Smith's knowledge and the respect that he commanded. He contributed over two hundred articles himself. This edition was also referred to as the "Scholars' Encyclopædia," and its popularity and impact can be illustrated with the fact that by the end of the nineteenth century, the publishers, Adam & Charles Black, sold nine thousand sets in Europe, and forty-five thousand in the United States (Sefton 2007: 301).

It was under his editorship that a fellow Scot, folklorist and ethnologist Andrew Lang (1844–1912), wrote the important contribution "Mythology" for volume 17 (published in 1884), the article that decisively argued *against* the philological and *for* the anthropological study of myth.[9] After moving to Cambridge,[10]

Figure 1.5. A portrait of Smith in 1876, drawn by George Reid. Family photos, courtesy of Astrid Hess. Reprinted with permission.

in 1884 Smith met another Scot, classicist James G. Frazer, and asked him to contribute the articles "Totem" and "Taboo" for the *Encyclopædia Britannica*.[11] Based on the work already published by McLennan, Smith (1886: 135) wrote about totem as "an animal (less often a plant); the kindred is of the stock of its totem; and to kill or eat the sacred animal is an impiety of the same kind with that of killing and eating a tribesman" (see also Smith 1914: 124ff.; and Cook 1902). However, he chose to ask Frazer to write these articles for the *Encyclopædia*.[12] In letter to the publishers, he wrote,

> I hope that Messrs. Black clearly understand that Totemism is a subject of growing importance, daily mentioned in the magazines and papers, but of which there is no good account anywhere—precisely one of those cases where we have an opportunity of getting ahead of every one and getting some reputation. There is no article in the volume for which I am more solicitous. I have taken much personal pains with it, guiding Frazer carefully in his treatment; and he has put about seven months' hard work on it to make it the standard article on the subject. (Smith, in Black and Chrystal 1912a: 494)

Smith and Frazer developed a very close friendship, and Frazer's biographer Robert Ackerman (1987: 161–162) hints that their relationship might have had some erotic elements. However, it was probably not a homosexual relationship in a way that it would be understood today, as it did not involve very much close physical contact.[13] They spent a lot of time together while they were both at Trinity College in Cambridge, and enjoyed long walks and dinners. It seems that Frazer was both impressed by Smith as a person and as an intellectual mentor. In retrospect, it also seems that Smith symbolized some kind of a father figure for him, even though he was only eight years older. Therefore, by distancing himself from Smith's theories in the early twentieth century, Frazer also committed some sort of "an Oedipal parricide" (Ackerman 2008: 77). On the other hand, perhaps his understanding of Smith's theories was incomplete, as Leach (1985: 238) observed in a chapter that he wrote about anthropology of religion: "Although he [Robertson Smith] was a major inspiration to Frazer, the latter never understood the significance of Smith's breakthrough from patchwork synthetic ethnography to sociology."

Smith's most important contributions to anthropology were published during this period: notably *Kinship and Marriage in Early Arabia* (1885), which was, at least in part, inspired by McLennan's ideas on totemism. At the very beginning of the book, he described the book's main purpose to be

> to collect and discuss the available evidence as to the genesis of the system of male kinship, with the corresponding laws of marriage and tribal organisation, which prevailed in Arabia at the time of Mohammed; the general result is that male kinship had been preceded by kinship through women only, and that all that can still be gathered as to the steps of the social evolution in which the change of kinship law is the central feature corresponds in the most striking manner with the general theory propounded, mainly on the basis of a study of modern rude societies, in the late J. F. McLennan's book on *Primitive Marriage*. (Smith 1907: xi)

Most of the arguments Smith had already developed in the article in the *Journal of Philology*, published five years earlier (Smith 1912a). This article was published at the height of the arguments expressed in his trial, and made his position, in view of the dominant Scottish Calvinist majority, indefensible.

> First, concerning marriage and the marriage laws in Israel, the views expressed are so gross and so fitted to pollute the moral sentiments of the community that they cannot be considered except within the closed doors of any court of this Church. Secondly, concerning animal worship in Israel, the views expressed by the Professor are not only contrary to the facts recorded and the statements made in Holy Scripture, but they are gross and sensual—fitted to pollute and debase public sentiment. Third, concerning the worship of God in Israel, and the law of that worship in the temple, and generally in the times of the Old Testament, the statements of the professor are not only contrary to all evidence, but they are also fitted to destroy all reverence for

God and for his Holy Word. (Mr. Macauly's addendum to the resolution of the meeting of 28 July 1881, in Black and Chrystal 1912a: 381–382; quoted in Livingstone 2004a: 2)

The first edition of the *Lectures on the Religion of the Semites* followed a few years later (1889). Between these two volumes, he wrote another extremely influential article, "Sacrifice," which was published in the *Encyclopædia Britannica* in 1886.

The *Lectures* book was the product of the first in a succession of three series of public talks given in response to the April 1887 invitation by the Burnett Trustees of the University of Aberdeen. Smith was asked to deliver lectures on "the primitive religions of the Semitic peoples, viewed in relation to other ancient religions, and to the spiritual religion of the Old Testament and Christianity."[14] The invitation was very important for Smith, as he was interested in comparing the data he already had with data about non-Semitic peoples. He clearly acknowledged in the preface what we would today call a "comparative method," mentioning "invaluable assistance from my friend, Mr. J. G. Frazer, who has given me free access to his unpublished collections on the superstitions and religious observances of primitive nations in all parts of the globe" (Smith 2002: xlvii).

According to Smith's biographers, the first two series of Burnett Lectures "were devoted to mythological matters and the main features of Semitic polytheism, and the third to Semitic views of the creation and government of the world" (Black and Chrystal 1912a: 535). The second series was delivered in March of 1890, but very little was known about it for almost a century. The general subject of the third and last series, delivered in the Marischal College on 10, 12, and 14 December 1891, was the "nature and origin of the gods of Semitic Heathenism, their relations to one another, the myths that surround them, and the whole subject of religious belief, so far as is not directly involved in the observances of daily religious life" (Black and Chrystal 1912a: 535; cf. Smith 1914, preface to the first edition). Unfortunately, illness prevented Smith from completing these other two series for publication. Only two weeks before his death, Smith completed revisions to his original *Lectures* manuscript, which he passed on to his friend John Sutherland Black (Smith 1914: xi).

This book remains one of the key texts for interpreting ancient Semitic sacrificial rituals and their integral beliefs. As a matter of fact, one of its commentators noted in his outline of the *Lectures* that "a unique combination of circumstances had brought the Burnett lecturer to the point where he was to give to the world a book which, in its range of learning, attention to detail, and power of argument has had few rivals before or since" (Rogerson 1979: 228).

The manuscript and all the records of the second and third series of lectures were long thought to have been lost. This was also assumed by Smith's biographers, J. S. Black and G. Chrystal (1912), and simply taken by scholars ever since as a fact. It seems that one of Smith's greatest regrets was realizing, as his health deteriorated, that he would not be able to prepare these two series of lectures for publication. The story about the second and third series of lectures changed dramatically almost a century after Smith's death, after John Day (who was at the time a fellow and tutor in theology at Lady Margaret Hall and lecturer in Old Testament at the University of Oxford) rediscovered the original notes for the manuscript in the early 1990s. In 1991, Day, with the help of Rachel Hart, an archivist at the University of Aberdeen, also discovered press reports of the original lectures, which had been published in the *Daily Free Press* and the *Aberdeen Journal*. These reports were also included in the subsequent publication of the second and third series (Day 1995). Although these two series were published from Smith's notes only, and without the extensive annotations and additional references that he would have included (so they should more accurately be referred to as primarily extensive *lecture notes*), they still represent an extraordinary scholarly achievement. Day's introduction to this short book was also published (although in an abbreviated form) in the volume that resulted from the William Robertson Smith Congress, organized by William Johnstone and held at King's College in Aberdeen on the occasion of the centenary of Smith's death, between 5 and 9 April 1994 (Johnstone 1995). As a final result of the publication of the second and third series of his lectures, a much more complete picture of W. R. Smith as a scholar emerged—as one of the greatest minds of his time. To give an example: some of the criticism directed at him after the publication of the first volume of *Lectures* was that he ignored the most recent archaeological and epigraphic (especially Assyrological) discoveries of the late nineteenth century. But these discoveries were not relevant for the topics that he was concerned with in the first series. The published text of the second and third series shows that he did take these discoveries into account, and that he was obviously very familiar with the work of leading scholars in the field, such as P. Jensen and E. Schrader and others. In his introduction, Day also noted that Smith could easily interpret the ancient Greek and Latin sources—providing additional arguments for his theories. One of the reviewers summarized as follows:

> This book is more than a mere snapshot of Victorian biblical scholarship at its height. Robertson Smith's encyclopedic command of Classical, Phoenician, Syriac, and Arabic sources, together with his unstated essentialist belief in the survival of Semitic religion across the centuries, has the combined effect of shifting the comparative perspective forward into the Hellenistic period and beyond. (Holloway 2000: 138)

Another one noted that these lectures are marks of an exceptional scholar. "His interest in the phenomenology of religion is everywhere evident, and his models are never superimposed on the evidence and never just theoretical in character. They are consistently relevant both culturally and historically" (Levine 1997: 617).

In 1883, Smith accepted Lord Almoner's Readership in Arabic at the University of Cambridge and became a fellow of Trinity College. Two years later, in 1885, he became a fellow of Christ's College (the same Cambridge college attended by men such as

John Milton and Charles Darwin before him), and a year later, University Librarian. He received honorary doctorates from the University of Aberdeen and the University of Strasbourg (Salmond 1894: 360). However, by this time, Smith's health was already rapidly declining (he was suffering from spinal tuberculosis), and he was additionally affected first by the death of his brother Herbert, in 1887, and then by his father's death, in 1890.[15] In 1889, he was appointed to the Sir Thomas Adams Chair of the Professor of Arabic, a post that he held until his death, at Cambridge, on 31 March 1894.

On the occasion of his death, the General Assembly of the Free Church of Scotland (the same institution that had tried him as a heretic during his lifetime) adopted a formal resolution stating that Smith's "intellectual energy and industry, his quick apprehension, his singular command of his varied knowledge, along with a rare power of clear and felicitous expression, combined to rank him among the most remarkable men of his time" (Black and Chrystal 1912a: 560).

Figure 1.6. Smith in his Cambridge office, around 1889. Family photos, courtesy of Astrid Hess. Reprinted with permission.

Figure 1.7. William Robertson Smith in 1893, photogravure by George Reid. Family photos, courtesy of Astrid Hess. Reprinted with permission.

NOTES

The epigraph is from Carswell 1927: 68.

1. This overview of his life is based on Black and Chrystal 1912a, with some additional information from Bryce 1903; Brown 1964; Beidelman 1974; Muilenberg in Smith 1969; Sefton 2004; and Hess, n.d. A complete list of Smith's works has been published by Brown (1964: appendix B). A bibliography of the publications related to his trial has been published by Beidelman (1974a: 85–92). There is also a very informative bilingual (English and German) website with a lot of easily accessible information about his life, set up by Mrs. Astrid Hess, great-granddaughter of Smith's sister, Alice—http://www.william-robertson-smith.net/index .htm (Hess, n.d.).

2. He was fifteen, and his brother George only thirteen years old. They were the two youngest students of that class, and won most of the bursaries for incoming students for that year. They came to Aberdeen accompanied by their two sisters, Mary Jane and Isabella. The girls went to school, but also "kept the house" for their brothers. Mary Jane contracted tuberculosis while taking care of her sick brother George, and passed away in 1864. George died a couple of weeks after Smith's graduation, in 1865 (Black 1900: 160).

3. A school of thought associated with the more scholarly (critical) approaches to the Bible, including comparative linguistic and historical approaches. It gained prevalence in Europe especially after the breakthroughs made by Immanuel Kant (1724–1804) and G. W. F. Hegel (1770–1831) in philosophy, but also following investigations and publications by Adolf Bastian (1826–1905) in ethnology. The most prominent British scholars who supported this new comparative approach were A. B. Davidson and T. K. Cheyne. For the examination of the relationship of the proponents of this approach and Smith, see Brown 1964 and Bailey 1970.

4. Wellhausen was one of the most important and most influential Orientalists of his time. After starting his career at Göttingen, he taught at the University of Greifswald (1872–1882); later he taught at Halle and Marburg, and finally settling back in Göttingen. Wellhausen's version of the "documentary hypothesis" about the origin of the Pentateuch/ Torah was the most influential theory on this topic throughout most of the twentieth century—right until 1970s. According to this hypothesis, books of the Pentateuch were not written by Moses, but were a result of different accounts that evolved from an oral tradition over the course of at least five centuries. Smith wrote the preface for the English language

translation of Wellhausen's major work, *Prolegomena zur Geschichte Israels*, in 1885 (Wellhausen 1899, 1973), noting that

> the history of Israel is part of the history of the faith by which we live, the New Testament cannot be rightly understood without understanding the Old, and the main reason why so many parts of the Old Testament are practically a sealed book even to thoughtful people is simply that they have not the historical key to the interpretation of that wonderful literature. (Smith, in Wellhausen 1973: viii).

5. It seems that a great part of his writing was meant to refute the theories put forth by another important ancestor of anthropology, Sir Henry Maine (1822–1888), but I cannot enter into the specifics of McLennan's criticism here.

6. Frazer published his four-volume *Totemism and Exogamy* in 1910, based on the material collected by researchers, ethnologists, ministers, and travelers in Melanesia and Australia. In this work, he explicitly rejected Smith's (as well as McLennan's) theories.

7. A detailed summary of some issues raised by the trial was provided by Bryce (1903: 313):

> The propositions he stated regarding the origin of the parts of the Old Testament, particularly the Pentateuch, excited alarm and displeasure in Scotland, where few persons had become aware of the conclusions reached by recent Biblical scholars in Continental Europe. The article was able, clear, and fearless, plainly the work of a master hand. The views it advanced were not for the most part due to Smith's own investigations, but were to be found in the writings of other learned men. Neither would they now be thought extreme; they are in fact accepted today by many writers of unquestioned orthodoxy in Britain and a (perhaps smaller) number in the United States.

8. For a more detailed account of this trial and all the circumstances surrounding it, cf. chapters 6–10 in Black and Chrystal 1912a. For a somewhat broader context, and with more details about the Free Church and its internal politics, see Glover 1954 and Riesen 1985.

9. It should be noted that Tylor, the only nineteenth-century scholar who dedicated his time exclusively to anthropology, also wrote eleven entries for this edition of *Encyclopædia Britannica*.

10. After the completion of the heresy trial, Smith was offered a job at Harvard University, but declined.

11. Frazer was also assigned the following entries: Penates, Priapus, Proserpina, Pericles, Theseus, and Thespiae (Boon 2008: 55).

12. It was under Smith's influence that Frazer developed his concepts of the sacrifice of divine kings. Frazer, of course, developed this idea in the completely opposite direction from Smith's ideas, as he wanted to demonstrate how myth formed a necessary (evolutionary) stage in the development of human understanding.

13. On the other hand, the fact is that he socialized almost exclusively with men, or, as noted in a moving obituary,

> He had the gift of attaching men closely, even fondly, to him, and he was never without associates, some of them younger than himself, not a few of them much older, men of ways of life, too, and professional avocations very different from his own, who clung to him not only because they honoured him for his great and varied abilities or sympathised with him in the causes which he championed, but because they valued him for his personal worth, his kindness, generosity, and loyalty. (Salmond 1894: 357)

14. In the formal letter of invitation to present a series of Burnett Lectures, dated 21 March 1887, Alexander Bain wrote to him:

> My Dear Dr. Smith,
>
> The Burnett Trustees meet on the 7th April, to choose the next Lecturer. A preparatory meeting was held a few weeks ago, which all but determined what is to be the result of the meeting on the 7th. . . . On the assumption that "History" should be the subject there was but one opinion expressed at the former meeting, namely, that you should be asked to give the course, i. e. be appointed Lecturer.
>
> . . . The Trustees would consider it far more important for the success of the Lecture, that the topic should be thoroughly congenial to yourself, than that they should suggest it. For the sake of coming to a conclusion, I will assume that it should refer to the old Semitic religions, or others related to them by way of derivation, contrast or otherwise. In short, taking a wide view of the Semitic family and their allies and foils, the question is how to carve out a rounded course of twelve lectures that would both interest the public, and give you full scope for all your freshest information and research: or for any further research that you would wish to enter upon so as to make the outcome (namely, a book) satisfactory and creditable both to yourself and us. Completeness and general interest might, of course, require compilation and exposition of matter already available, to be supported with whatever novelty you could yourself impart. (Anon., n.d.)

15. His biographers note that he took special care to see that his mother would be provided for after his father's death.

CHAPTER 2

SMITH'S TRAVELS AND ETHNOGRAPHIES

● ● ●

Behind us on the horizon was the crescent moon, and over her the morning star, shining as it never shines in northern latitudes, "Lucifer the son of the dawn" floating in a mist of faint morning light, like an infant deity in the lap of his mother.

—William Robertson Smith, in the *Scotsman*

Unlike many of his contemporaries, who wrote extensively about peoples and cultures that they had never seen, Smith was able to make several trips to, and to spend extensive periods of time in, the geographic area of his expertise. This should be taken into consideration when one reads references to him as an "armchair anthropologist" (Parman 1995: 264).[1] In the winter of 1879/1880, he visited Cairo (Egypt) and Palestine. As he was suspended from teaching during the heresy trial, this trip was unexpectedly extended to six months and enabled him to improve his Arabic, as well as to collect a great deal of what we would today call "ethnographic information." His relatively dark complexion, the fact that he wore native clothes, and his excellent command of Arabic enabled him to blend in easily with people and make friends. Smith returned to the Middle East in 1880/1881, and then traveled extensively through the Arabian Peninsula, and all the way to Suez, spending two months at Jeddah and visiting Palestine, Syria, and Tunis (Smith 1912b). He again traveled to the

Middle East in the winter of 1890/1891—that time primarily for health reasons.

Letters from the first trip were published in the *Scotsman*. Smith traveled via Sicily, where he was especially impressed by the remnants of ancient Greek culture. His interest and descriptions of various ancient monuments, as well as comparative remarks about classical architectural styles, probably influenced some scholars to also refer to him as a "Biblical archæologist" (for example, Freud 2001: 154). It seems that his fascination for "survivals" of ancient traits was already formed by this time.

Of the Greek cities of Sicily Syracuse is beyond question the most interesting. Its historical importance extends over the longest time; it was in its palmy days the greatest of all Hellenic cities, and above all it was the scene of one of the most tragic and decisive conflicts of the world's history. Before Syracuse the long struggle of the Ionic and Doric races for supremacy was decided, and the traveller who visits the spot with Thucydides in his hand can still trace each step of the long and bitter fight in the unchanging topographical features of the hills that rise above the great haven. But after Syracuse, Acragas holds a foremost place in early Sicilian history. Its natural features are not inferior in interest, and the magnificent line of temples which still crowns the ancient wall facing the Mediterranean is without parallel among Grecian ruins. Here, better than in any other place, the traveller can stimulate his imagination to realise, without any excessive effort, the fairest developments of Dorian civilisation. In Greece and in Asia Minor the Ionians hold the first place. But in Sicily we see the Dorians at their best . . . . The repulse of Carthaginians by Theron of Acragas is a worthy companion piece to the repulse of Xerxes by Themistocles of Athens. The battle of Himera and the battle of Salamis can never be dissociated in the history of the liberation of Hellas from barbarians; and at Acragas, as at Athens, the victory ushered in a period of great prosperity, in which the city attained the beauty and glory of which many vestiges still remain. (Letter in the *Scotsman*, 5 December 1879)

Smith goes on to provide a detailed description of the ruins of Acragas, including the amphitheater, temples to Heracles and Zeus, and also the place which was the location of the temple of the goddess Athena, probably confirming the militaristic ambitions of the ancient inhabitants of Sicily. He remained completely enchanted by the place, writing, "The whole situation is such that one knows not whether to admire it most for strength or for beauty" (Letter in the *Scotsman*, 5 December 1879). Specific places were of great interest to Smith, as he mentioned, speaking of "Semitic heathenism" in the third series of his Burnett Lectures: "The energy of the god had its centre at the sanctuary where a holy fountain or a stream or grave was revered as instinct with divine life; it was here that the worshippers appeared before their god with gestures of adoration and gifts of homage" (in Day 1995: 63). The comparative perspective is very important here, as Smith wanted to understand the development of religious ideas in different cultures. "All the divine powers that preside over nature and human life were represented in the Hellenic pantheon, and within his own sphere each god had a world-wide sway" (in Day 1995: 62).

Upon the arrival to Cairo, Smith first observes, in his letter, how people live, especially with regard to general economic conditions, noting that the last harvest was good ("things are finally looking better in Egypt"), and explains different aspects that affect the local economy. But he is also very much interested in the feelings and wishes of ordinary people, especially some recent political changes (change of the local governor):

Next to the good harvest and the good Nile, the Egyptians are generally congratulating themselves on the change of their ruler. The intensity with which Ismail Pasha was hated, the way in which he had come to be regarded as a very incarnation of selfish and heartless tyranny, was little understood in Europe; for the timid Egyptian, always in terror of

the numerous spies that were on the watch, scarcely dared
to whisper his feelings even to himself. (Letter in the *Scotsman*, 8 December 1879)

When he traveled to Alexandria, Smith was also able to meet
with some local officials (and seemed quite unimpressed by
them), as well as see some ancient ruins, which continued to fas-
cinate him. In his letter, he advises that "a great deal could be
done for Egyptian archaeology by anyone visiting the ruins of
the Delta in summer. At that season one could get antiques with
certain knowledge where they came from—a knowledge which
makes all the difference between a collection of mere curiosities
and serviceable archaeological material. And besides this, large
and interesting stone remains would be found exposed, affording
inscriptions of historical value" (Letter in the *Scotsman*, 13 December 1879). His interest is both historical—trying to assess the
antiquity of different monuments—and practical, as he is interested in what his interlocutors think of stories about the ancient
Egyptian pharaohs as recounted in the Torah.

During this leg of the journey, he was also able to observe
some aspects of the changes in settlement patterns that were
slowly taking place:

The Gawâbis are just passing from the Nomad to the sed-
entary life. Their encampment is already a kind of village,
in which the Bedouin tents are pitched side by side with
huts of brick like those of the Fellah. The great Sheikh has
a very good house, and though 'Abd-el-Hamîd entertained
us in a large tent, part of the family were in a hut close by,
in which, if we pleased, we might have slept. But a rug on
the sand, even if half-a-dozen Arabs and a calf shared the
tent, was much to be preferred to a foul and stuffy closet;
so after supper our Sheikh had to pull down the curtain,
behind which the women have their quarters, and pack off
his harîm to the hut. In a few years the encampment will
consist entirely of huts, which are gradually increasing in
number, but as yet it is not recognized as a village, and

has no local name. (Letter in the *Scotsman*, 13 December 1879)

Smith the missionary, somewhat idealistic and perhaps naïve, with acute awareness of the importance of economic conditions in which people live, but with the strong hint of someone on the "civilizing quest" (clearly positioned against "the conservatism of the East"), comes out most clearly in the following lines, written during his brief stay in Suez:[2]

> The plainest lesson enforced by what we saw at Tariyeh and among the Arabs, is the utter inefficacy of great material constructions, like the railway, to effect any improvement on the condition of the people. We had a philosopher in Cairo the other day, the reputed head of advanced English thinkers, who was loud in praise of railways and steam-engines as the one means to raise the people from their present condition of Oriental barbarism. I should have liked to take him down to Tariyeh and show him how completely all these things pass over the masses without power to touch their life or alleviate their real miseries. . . . It is from below, not from above, that the East must be developed. (Letter in the *Scotsman*, 20 December 1879)

Smith and his companions crossed the Red Sea on 28 December, arriving in Suâkin. After describing different ports and providing details about their locations, capacities, etc., Smith gives a lengthy (and very detailed) description of local plants and animals, as well as birds and even butterflies in the area. The travelers were also interested in animals that could be hunted for meals, but Smith wrote, "Of larger game we saw at a distance the gazelle and the ariel, but these shy creatures did not let us within shot" (letter in the *Scotsman*, 10 January 1880). There were no permanent inhabitants in the area, but Smith left the description of the nomads that he encountered. His general fascination with nomadic peoples (as people who were supposed to be closer to nature and leading simpler but richer lives) is clearly expressed in the following lines:

The country is visited from time to time by the Nomads of Suâkin, several groups of whom I met tending magnificent camels, which being used almost exclusively as milkers, and seldom having a pack saddle on their backs, have far finer appearance than the mangey camels of Egypt and Arabia. The shepherds were all of the true Hadendoa type—an Ethiopian race, according to ethnologists, tall and well built, with regular and pleasing features, and reddish brown complexion. Their dress is a huge white wrapper disposed in graceful folds so as to cover the whole person. Their most striking characteristic, however, is the enormous bush of hair which projects, umbrella like, on all sides of the head, and forms a completed protection from the sun. They are very proud of this ornament, and though our shepherds lacked the refinement of mutton grease and hair powder, employed by the dandies of the town, the native comb, a short pointed stick, was worn in correct style, stuck through the mass of hair above the forehead. (Letter in the *Scotsman*, 10 January 1880)

Although unimpressed with the port of Suâkin ("the town proves to be not so well built as it appeared at first sight"), Smith still admired "the life of the streets." And in order to fully appreciate the life of the streets, one must pass through the local bazaar and get to a newly constructed causeway:

In the morning the causeway is occupied by a train of water-carriers, chiefly women, and all day long a group of delightfully hideous negresses, their wrists and ankles covered with silver rings and a small jewel of gold in the right nostril, are squatted about the causeway-head, keeping guard over a pile of leather water-bottles. . . . You cannot wish to see stouter or better made men than these fellows [Hadendoa drivers], whose glossy skins and well-filled forms show that their diet of *dura* (sorghum) and milk agrees well with them. These two elements compose the food of the whole countryside. (Letter in the *Scotsman*, 10 January 1880)

From Suâkin, Smith traveled to Jeddah, arriving there on 11 January. From there he continued to Hijaz, the journey covered in much more details and observations. They were preserved in a series of eleven letters published between March and June 1880 in the *Scotsman*, and later reprinted as a separate chapter in a volume edited by Black and Chrystal (Smith 1912b). In this ethnographic account, Smith again demonstrates great knowledge of the countries that he traveled through, and understanding of the customs of the people inhabiting them, but I will discuss his observations in more details in the next chapter. Unfortunately, at this time he was also a prisoner of the prejudices of his time, quite happy with his own Britishness (Smith 1912b: 493, 500; he actually refers to the country and culture he comes from as "English" although proudly referring to himself as an Aberdonian), and was not particularly well disposed toward Islam (511). In regard to the distribution of Christian books in the area, Smith noted that "in the interests of civilisation and of that progress which is seriously retarded by the current Moslem notion that their dry and barren literature is the most perfect that can be considered, it is heartily to be desired that a door should be opened to the circulation of Christian literature" (566–567)—because he believed that, among other things, "the Koran is the bulwark of all the prejudices and social backwardness in the East" (568).

However, it also seems that Smith gradually changed the way in which he was referring to Islam, as exemplified in the correspondence with his fellow traveler and compatriot Sir Richard Francis Burton (1821–1890). For example, after a warning from Burton, he actually deleted some of the more contentious expressions from the subsequent editions of his books. For example, Burton warned Smith against using the word "impostor" to criticize the transmission of a particular story in Islamic tradition—"Mohammed was no more than Paul, Luther or Calvin" (quoted in Booth 2009: 280). As a result of his criticism, Smith significantly revised some parts of the text in the next edition of *The Old Testament in the Jewish Church*. This fact—that Smith was ready to reconsider his opinions and accept criticism—should be considered when one encounters charges such as the one of "Orientalism" that critics such as Said (1995) later used against him. These charges were mentioned as one of the most important facts about Smith in the editorial of a special issue of the journal about Smith (Craig 2008: v).[3]

The same charges were also mentioned in one of the contributions to the William Robertson Smith Congress, when American anthropologist Susan Parman (1995: 264) claimed that Smith was "applying J. F. McLennan's evolutionary Orientalisms," and that his anthropological ideas "belong to the archaic formulations of nineteenth-century Victorian imperialism." I will leave the alleged connection with the "nineteenth-century Victorian imperialism" aside for the moment—especially as there are no data to support such an accusation. However, the charge of "Orientalism" is much more important and potentially more damaging, as it belongs to the register of serious accusations brought against anthropologists (as well as social scientists in general), especially frequent in the last fifty years. Contrary to what Said alleged in his important, influential, and widely quoted book, it should be pointed out that, for example, another anthropologist, Jonathan Skinner, contextualized Smith's alleged "Orientalism" in the paper delivered at the very same William Robertson Smith Congress in which Parman participated. As put by Skinner (1995: 380), "To define the Semitic people, Smith made careful examination of Oriental languages and cultures. He took Arabia as his starting point and delimited a region of Semitic speech spreading 'out round the margin of the Syrian desert till it strikes the natural boundaries, the Mediterranean, Mount Taurus, and the mountains of Armenia and Iran.'" Skinner (1995: 378–379) convincingly argues that, despite his prejudices (some of which I also just referred to above), Smith set out to provide a critical, scholarly study, clearly situating himself "as a modernist."[4] This positions his style in a completely different register to the one used by Said. It also paints a very different image than the one that is to be found in Said (1995: 234–236). As a matter of fact, "Smith also devoted much of his energy to reforming past Orientalist fictions and received doctrines by privileging Orientalist knowledge gained from his first-hand ethnographic experiences"

(Skinner 1995: 381). In any case, it would seem odd that some-one who was prejudiced against Islam (as claimed by Said) would at the same time consider that Arabic was (most likely) closest to the language that God spoke (Burkitt 1894; also quoted by John-stone 1995).[5]

In his detailed analysis of Smith's travelogue from the 1880 journey through the Arabian Peninsula, David Livingstone also convincingly argues that Smith was never engaged in some form of Orientalizing "othering." Rather, according to Livingstone (2004b: 654), this journey is better understood as a voyage of self-discovery, as well as a pilgrimage to the roots of Christianity:

> In seeking to determine the structure and meaning of the "fundamental institutions" of the ancient Semites, and in scouring the Arabian world for echoes of kinship forms and customary rituals still reverberating from a world long forgot, Smith was in pursuit of nothing less than the cultural foundations of Western Christianity and the ultimate grounds of his own deepest convictions.

Smith became an established and well-respected academic in the years following the publication of Tylor's magnum opus, *Primitive Culture* (1871), and he shared some developmental perspectives with his contemporaries (see Smith 1914: 2; Jones 1984: 50–51).[6] Some degree of evolutionism was an integral part of all the British scientific perspectives at this time—especially in the years immediately following the publication of Darwin's *On the Origin of Species*—and even more after the publication of *The Descent of Man* (Darwin 1871).[7] On the other side of the Atlantic, the most influential nineteenth-century anthropologist, Lewis Henry Morgan, was an evolutionist.[8] In the introduction to his most famous work, Morgan (1877: 4, 12) claims that there are "several lines of progress toward the primitive ages of mankind," and only through carefully examining these, can one understand the formation of human societies, from "savagery," through "barbarism," and finally into the stage of "civilization." This was in tune with the whole expansion of the settlement toward the western part of the United States, as well as with the idea of American "manifest destiny." On the other hand, the language that he uses does not invoke race or class—Morgan believed in equality and human dignity, and he lived his life in accordance with his convictions. As noted by Virginia Dominguez (2018: 10) at a conference celebrating Morgan's bicentenary, "progress and hierarchy were common assumptions" at this time. In order to understand the whole context of Morgan's work, one should be aware of the important role that he played in helping the Seneca, as noted in an excellent recent study of his work:

> During his lifetime, the remaining Native Americans were forcibly removed from their homes and driven to lands of different ecological conditions, where they were made to earn their living using agricultural techniques that were full of risks and unfamiliar to them. Most of the displaced Amerindians died or became destitute. Morgan tried to organize resistance against these policies of his government. His active interference saved some Iroquois from removal and death. (Pfeffer 2019: 186)

However, the situation in which early British scholars at the same time found themselves—especially when considering issues related to faith—was slightly different. For example, Smith firmly believed that Christianity (especially as exemplified in his own brand of Scottish Presbyterianism, of the Free Church of Scotland) was the highest possible form of religion, although he did give some credit to the ancient Semitic peoples (especially Jews) for being essentially on the right track. Both Arabs and Jews, he felt, represented peoples whose beliefs and rituals went through the stages in the development through which Christian religion had to pass as well, so it was very important to understand these developmental stages and these religions (as well as other, "primitive" ones, which could be successfully contrasted with them) in order to fully understand Christianity (Smith 1892: 57, 274). In one of his early papers ("Animal Tribes and Animal Worship . . ."), Smith provides his reasoning for adopting this developmental perspective: "I start from Arabia, because the facts referring to that country belong to a more primitive state of society than existed in Israel at the time when the Old Testament was written, and because in Arabia before Islam we find a condition of pure polytheism, and not as in Israel the struggle between spiritual religion and the relics of ancestral heathenism (Josh. xxiv. 2)" (in Black and Chrystal 1912b: 459).

At the same time, Smith was convinced that by considering concepts such as sacrifice among the "positive religions," one would more likely be able to understand the role that sacrifice played among the more ancient, "primitive religions," which provide the foundations for Christianity as he knew and practiced it (Schmidt 1994: 132). Paul Radin (1937: 183) later claimed that anthropological study of sacrifice in religion actually begins with Smith, and that "his famous theory of the sacramental meal by which the community and the gods are united in a common bond, has influenced all subsequent theoretical inquiries." This was related to some important distinctions—some of which, as noted before, had made it into other scholars' works. For example, in his discussion of the differentiation between the holy and the unclean, Smith (1969: 152–153) also noted the importance of Christianity for recognizing holiness "as exclusively spiritual" (Segal 2008b: 19). This was going back to his comments (in the conclusion of the same 1880 article, "Animal Worship and Animal Tribes . . .") that "our investigations appear to confirm this judgment, and to show that the superstitions with which the spiritual religion had to contend were not one whit less degrading than those of the most savage nations" (Smith 1912b: 483).

NOTES

The epigraph is from Smith's letter in the *Scotsman*, 20 December 1879.
  1. It is very difficult to understand the consistent popularity of the phrase "armchair anthropologist" in the texts referring to the history of anthropology. This terminology is used to symbolically express the dyadic boundary between "old-fashioned" and "proper" anthropology, which

insists on fieldwork—and like all "us vs. them" artificial distinctions, it has some problems, and some of the criticism directed at early anthropologists is factually inaccurate. Where some of the late-nineteenth and early-twentieth-century "usual suspects" are concerned, it is a well-known fact that Tylor traveled to Mexico (which actually inspired his interest in ethnographic research), and that he did some field research in the U.S. Southwest, as well as in London (Holdsworth 2006). Frazer traveled to Greece on several occasions (after all, he was a classicist), and conducted research there, and was also invited to join Haddon and Rivers in the 1898 Cambridge University Torres Strait expedition, but had to decline (Ackerman 1987).

2. Old prejudices die hard, as one could see from this observation from the *Lectures*: "Nothing appeals so strongly as religion to the conservative instincts; and conservatism is the habitual attitude of Orientals" (Smith 2002: 4).

3. As this was a special issue of the journal, with excellent contributions by notable scholars, it is somewhat peculiar that these charges were just mentioned, without checking if they were accurate.

4. Booth (1999) provides a specific context (and brilliantly describes a social milieu of nineteenth-century Scotland) for the development of Smith's ideas, especially with regard to his interest in science, belief in human rationality, and his adherence to rigorous scientific methodology.

5. See also the important examples that Maier (2009: 173–174) provides—which clearly point to the fact that Smith cannot be accused of having racial prejudices.

6. The following lines from the *Lectures* provide a very good example: "Savages, we know, are not only incapable of separating in thought between phenomenal and noumenal existence, but habitually ignore the distinctions, which to us seem obvious, between organic and inorganic nature, or within the former region between animals and plants" (Smith 1914: 85–86).

7. With the possible exception of Lang who, while drawing heavily on Tylor's work in his earlier publications (1885, 1887), was very critical of both Tylor and Frazer in his later works, such as *Magic and Religion* (1901).

Also, there is a question of whether Sir Edward Burnett Tylor should actually be simply labeled an "evolutionist"—at least as the term is taken to mean today—given his frequent criticism of the prejudices and misconceptions against the "primitives," as well as his comparative approach that was in tune with the universalist tendencies of many other nineteenth-century scholars. For example, Ingold (2004) notes in his lecture that there were actually two different Tylors (as Tylor modified his views over time)—and, for example, that the one who wrote the *Primitive Culture* was definitively *not* an evolutionist. It seems that his comparative approach was at least as important as the belief in the general progress of societies and their institutions; this type of comparativism was also characteristic for Morgan and Frazer. So, again, clear distinctions are not always possible, and one needs to understand and interpret writings of past scholars with consideration of the specific time periods in which they lived and the context in which their ideas were formulated and published, as well as the fact that they did not necessarily hold the same views throughout their careers.

8. Morgan (1818–1881) was an American lawyer, one of the key figures instrumental in the establishment of anthropology in the United States. He was especially important because of the detailed studies of the Iroquois, conducted with his famous collaborator and friend, Seneca attorney and engineer Ely Parker (1828–1895). Parker's Seneca name was Ha-sa-no-an-da. Morgan's book, *League of the Ho-de'-no-sau-nee, or Iroquois*, published in 1851, was the first ethnography of a Native American nation (or "tribe"). Morgan was very much and very actively dedicated to the welfare of the Senecas, so from the contemporary perspective he could also be perceived as an early example of an "engaged anthropologist" (Pfeffer 2019: 13–15, 186). With his studies of kinship and family, and his insistence on the evolutionary progress of human societies, Morgan influenced economists and political scientists, such as Friedrich Engels (1820–1895) and Karl Marx (1818–1883). Engels was especially responsible for the favorable twentieth-century assessment of Morgan's views in the socialist countries of Europe, especially after World War II; as summed up by Pfeffer (2019: 18), "Only Marxists have given unqualified and lasting support to Morgan's theories." It is interesting to note that Morgan organized a meeting with his British colleagues (including McLennan) in London in 1871 (Pfeffer 2019: 118).

CHAPTER 3

A JOURNEY IN THE HIJAZ

●　●　●

Though the people of Arabia, the genuine Bedouins, are believed to have changed little or nothing in their mode of life since the days of the Shepherd Kings of Abraham's time, waves of political and religious agitation have occasionally rippled over one part or another of the ancient peninsula. Seemingly they make as little permanent impression on the undercurrent of Bedouin life, as do the waves of the sea on its immutable whole, so that the accounts of the earlier chroniclers of Arabian life and manners agree in a singular manner with the descriptions of contemporary visitors.
　　—Thomas Stevens, in Taylor's *Travels in Arabia*

As noted in the previous chapter, Smith first traveled extensively around the Arabian peninsula in 1880. This is also the time period from which one of his most famous images, in which he is dressed in Arab clothes ("Abdullah Efendi" was a nickname that his guides gave him), comes from (see figure 3.1). The image today serves as a reminder of a nineteenth-century scholar "going native"—or simply as a demonstration of Smith's desire and ability to better understand the culture that he was studying. It all depends on one's perspective. Details from his journeys were published in the series of letters in the *Scotsman*. Today these letters can also be seen as an example of an early ethnographic account—with the narrator (Smith) firmly positioned within it. They are much more than descriptions of a journey into a different area of the world. They provide very good description of

Smith's travels and events that marked particular stages of the journey, but also some important notes about the customs of the people ("tribes") that he and his traveling companions met on the way. Especially interesting are his observations about patriarchy as a recent phenomenon (i.e., a major cultural shift that came as a result of the Islamization of the societies), and here one can recognize the influence of McLennan—but I will discuss this influence in the next chapter.

By the time of Smith's travels, European explorations of the Arabian peninsula (which was at the time part of the Ottoman Empire) were already taking place. Swiss Orientalist Johann Ludwig Burckhardt (1784–1817) traveled extensively through the region in the early nineteenth century, visiting both Jedda and Taif. In the process, Burckhardt also rediscovered the Nabathean ruins of Petra (in today's Jordan), and left an impressive body of work (notes and observations), which was published after his death. Among the more colorful characters, English explorer and adventurer Charles Montagu Doughty (1843–1926) was noted for openly declaring himself an infidel in the holiest Muslim city of Mecca. Smith would later be in touch with another fascinating character from this period, Sir Richard Burton—but even before his travels he was already able to read about Burton's exploits in a fascinating overview of Western travelers in the region since 1730, *Travels in Arabia*, the first edition of which was published in 1872 (Taylor 1892). Much later, some interesting accounts about the "unknown tribes" living in the southern part of Arabia were published by Bertram Thomas (1929), including ones that featured measurements of physical characteristics of the local population (Thomas 1932)—in line with the strange anthropometric tendencies of the time. Several of the early accounts, including Burton's, are briefly presented in an informative anthology edited by Nash (2009).

The western part of the Arabian Peninsula, Hijaz (also spelled Hejaz, or Hedjaz in different texts), was ruled by the Hashemites, and it is the area where Islam arose. The Prophet Muhammad was born in Mecca, and he was buried in Medina (also spelled Madina, or al-Madinah), which was also where the first Islamic

Figure 3.1. "Abdullah Efendi"—Smith during his voyage to Egypt and the Arabian Peninsula in 1880. Illustration from the photo by A. Dew Smith, in Black and Chrystal 1912a. Work in public domain.

state was formed. This part of the Arabian Peninsula became independent immediately after World War I, but was conquered by the House of Saud in 1924. However, it was fully integrated in the newly formed Kingdom of Saudi Arabia only in 1932 (Yamani 2009: xiii, 9–11). In her detailed account of the region and its sociocultural complexities, British-Saudi anthropologist Mai Yamani provides numerous examples of how this conquest left many issues open, and that a distinctive local identity can still be observed on multiple levels. Even though the geographical identity has been erased (Hijaz is now simply part of the so-called Western Province, so it can be regarded as a social construct), many of the customs that Saudis use are actually considered by Hijazis as their own (Yamani 2009: 13–15). This puts Hijaz in the interesting position of being both a symbol of the past ("tradition") and at the same time a crucial component of the formation of the modern Kingdom of Saudi Arabia, with all of its entangled sociocultural identities.

In his scathing criticism of William Robertson Smith, Edward Said (1995: 235) describes him as "a crucial link in the intellectual chain connecting the White-Man-as-expert to the modern Orient." According to this line of criticism, Orientalist excesses in the twentieth century were only made possible with the help and authority of someone like Smith. I will not discuss here the fact that from Said's references it appears that he read only the two books edited by Black and Chrystal, as well as *Kinship and Marriage in Early Arabia* (Smith 1907)—so his understanding of Smith's ideas is at least based on very limited evidence. He obviously remained completely unaware of the discussions initiated by McLennan and Morgan (which I will discuss further in the next chapter), to which *Kinship and Marriage in Early Arabia* owes its very existence. Therefore, he was completely unaware of the social, historical, and methodological context or complexity of Smith's work. Unfortunately, all of this did not prevent him from claiming that "the power of Smith's work is its plainly radical demythologizing of the Semites" (Said 1995: 235). Said (1995: 236) goes as far as to claim that, if one takes Smith seriously, "Islam can thus be characterized as totalitarian"—a claim difficult to be corroborated by anyone who has actually read Smith's books or articles. I already referred to Skinner's (1995) observation that Said seemed to expect that Smith shared his (late-twentieth-century) "post-modernism." On the other hand, Said's general hostility to anthropology and anthropologists is well documented

(Lewis 2007). However, there is also a fundamental misunderstanding between the different worldviews,[1] exemplified in the following lines:

> Like Burton and Charles Doughty before him, Smith voyaged in the Hejaz . . . . Arabia has been an especially privileged place for the Orientalist, not only because Muslims treat Islam as Arabia's *genius loci*, but also because the Hejaz appears historically as barren and retarded as it is geographically; the Arabian desert is thus considered to be a locale about which one can make statements regarding the past in exactly the same form (and with the same content) that one makes them regarding the present. In the Hejaz you can speak about Muslims, modern Islam, and primitive Islam without bothering to make distinctions. To this vocabulary devoid of historical grounding, Smith was able to bring the cachet of additional authority provided by his Semitic studies. (Said 1995: 235)

Said's contempt for Hijaz is difficult to understand, given his lack of actual experience of the region. Perhaps coming from an urban, intellectual milieu prevented him from appreciating something that seemed so distant (and physically different, especially in terms of geography). The study of an important contemporary anthropologist, Mai Yamani (someone who actually spent some time living in the region and studying it), presents a very different perspective: the image of a culturally complex and historically significant region—the site of events that played a crucial role in the development of modern Middle East, as well as the establishment of the Saudi state. The contrast and the fundamental difference in perspective is obvious when one compares Said's description ("historically as barren and retarded as it is geographically") to the opening paragraph of Yamani's (2009: 1) book:

> The area of the Arabian peninsula known as Hijaz takes its name—and its character—from *al-Hijaz*, the "barrier"

formed by the great escarpment that rises to the south like a wall behind Mecca and runs parallel to the coast as far as Yemen. Historically both nomadic and settled communities inhabited the area, but Hijaz's urban centres—the Islamic holy cities of Mecca and Medina, as well as Jeddah and Taif—have dominated its development during the past fourteen centuries. Looking not inland but towards the sea, the Hijaz gained an international reputation for trade and as the focus of the Islamic *hajj* (pilgrimage), which contributed to its relative economic prosperity and enhanced its political significance.

Very far from being "barren and retarded" as described by Said, Smith (1912b: 484), writing almost a century earlier, was fascinated by Hijaz and referred to it as definitively worth seeing, even though "to the curious traveller the upper country will repay a visit; but the journey is toilsome and costly, and hardly recommended to any one who has not some knowledge of Arabic." The journey, however, comes with many rewards, primarily in experiencing a fascinating and rich world of magnificent scenery, outstanding hospitality, and some very interesting customs. Some of these were very important for Smith's future work, especially regarding kinship and social organization, and it is easy to see how some of his observations were influenced by what he had already read in McLennan's *Primitive Marriage*. Some were already included in his 1880 article in the *Journal of Philology*, and others were more clearly formulated in *Kinship and Marriage in Early Arabia*.

Smith's journey to Taif is described in great detail, beginning with his traveling companions—who they were, how they looked, what kind of stories they liked to tell when sitting around the fire in the evenings. There is a description of the places they went through on the way, including description of trees, especially acacias (Smith 1912b: 524). Knowledge of vegetation was important, for, as he noted, "I found various trees and shrubs to have a very well defined local distribution, so that my men would often identify a place by specifying what grew at it" (524). There are also descriptions of different meals, and customs associated with preparing them, as well as a brief discussion of Bedouin "superstitions about animals." As monkeys are believed to have been men before (in an earlier era), their flesh is not eaten (530–531). There are also stories related to the particular locations that they go through during the journey:

> We passed several objects to which legends are attached— first, a great stone by the roadside, which is said to have been lifted by a girl, a story which educed the information that the trial of strength by lifting stones which Jerome describes as practiced in Palestine is still known among the Arabs. Then on the mountain top to our right a natural obelisk was pointed out as a girl who had been turned into rock for casting a stone at one of the ancient prophets. (Smith 1912b: 537–538)

Finally, the traveling party arrived at their destination: "Tâif . . . is a small city, populous, irrigated by sweet waters, with a salubrious climate, abounding in crops, with ample fields especially rich in grapes, and famed for its raisins. Most of the fruit for Mecca is brought from it." (Smith 1912b: 550–551) On the other hand, Smith mentions a tradition (which he judges to be "absurd") according to which the city was "supernaturally conveyed from Damascus to the Hejâz at the prayer of Abraham," and says it is "a story which means nothing more than that Tâif, with its orchards, is the Damascus of the Hejâz, and a city of unknown antiquity" (553). After a detailed description of the city and its setup, including comparative observations about the construction of houses and mosques in different Arabian towns, Smith provides a description of the family of his host, Muhtesib Hosein, including his wives and his children. Readers are provided with an insight into the family life of a middle-class local family, including some specific customs related to marriage and dowry. He describes the hospitality as "unsparing and a little burdensome" (568)—it seems that they were very keen to have him well fed, but Smith felt that if he would eat the three meals per day that were expected, given the duration of the meals and the quantity of food, he could have no time to do anything else. Still, by skipping some meals, he "made most of his opportunities," and was able to collect "a good deal of information about the tribes' customs" (568). Smith devotes several pages to the description of the political organizations of different "tribes" in the area (571–580). There are depictions of local warriors and "turbulent tribes" that include some fantastic elements—for example: "All accounts agree that the Qahtan [one of the "turbulent tribes" that he discusses in this letter] are very savage, but the practice of drinking the blood of their enemies in time of war, with which they are generally credited, is perhaps now obsolete" (574).

Although admitting that he could not immediately see all the distinctive marks of particular tribal groups ("the cut of his sandals, the way in which long black locks hang behind the ear—in one tribe plaited, in another free—the length of the dirk, and so forth" [576]), Smith was still able to notice differences between them in the different types of weapons, primarily lances, that they used. There are also important observations on kinship patterns ("patriarchal system of society"), as well as a remark "that polyandria once prevailed in Arabia, and traces of this practice and of female kinship are to be found to a comparatively late date" (577–578), but I will discuss this further in the next chapter. These patterns will form an important part of his 1885 book on kinship and marriage, but the concept is also mentioned in the *Religion of the Semites*: "The conception of goddess-mother was not unknown, and seems to be attached to cults which go back to the ages of polyandry and female kinship" (Smith 2002: 56).

"Arabian customs" are the topic of the tenth letter, and Smith is especially interested in the blood feud, retaliation, and war. He refers to retaliation as "the most important of all Arabic principles," which also "received the sanction of religion under Islam" (Smith 1912b: 581). However, among the Bedouins, it is more ancient. Smith believed that the rules of blood feud and retaliation led to lesser casualties at times of war.

Generally speaking, an Arab invasion is a mere foray. The invaders scatter, attack the villages, drive off booty, and engage in skirmishes. The fire-arms of the Bedouins are fit only for irregular warfare—huge matchlocks, longer than their bearers, which can be fired with effect only from an ambush. In this way of fighting few lives are lost. It is more profitable to capture an enemy and hold him for ransom. To kill more of the enemy than is requisite to square accounts is very unwise, for when peace is made the balance of blood must be accounted for either in lives or money. (Smith 1912b: 584)

He also claimed that there was a humane side of the warring practices, and that side was "the respect paid to women and children, who are never harmed; yet the women are very bold, and are the first to stir on the men to battle. In the campaign, and even in the heat of the fight, the women follow their husbands or brothers, carrying water to the combatants, urging on laggards, and striking their cymbals over a victory" (Smith 1912b: 584).

Smith concludes this part of his observations by noting the differences in marital customs between different "tribes." He was told by Mustafa Pasha, the Wâly (governor) of Yemen[2] that "the Bedouins of Yemen have various traditional usages which they know to be inconsistent with Mohammedan orthodoxy, and are therefore careful to conceal them from the Turks" (Smith 1912b: 586). There was, however, a particular custom that was allowed, as unusual as it seemed:

The 'Aseer Arabs are accustomed to contract marriages of a temporary character by verbal agreement. The so-called marriage may endure but a day. It is, in fact, no more than a nominal contract to avoid the name of immorality. With this it naturally goes that no weight is laid on the chastity of unmarried women. . . . The Wâly tells me further that not only in Yemen, but among some of the tribes of the Syrian desert, the wife claims the right to leave her husband at will and take another spouse, and also that it is a recognized practice for husbands among some of the latter tribes . . . to make an exchange of wives. All these are obvious remains of early polyandria, and confirm the observation that the introduction of Islam was marked by great social reforms, of which we know but little, but which, in all probability, were at least as momentous as the innovations in religion which are generally regarded as forming the essence of Mohammedanism. (Smith 1912b: 584)

Said (1995: 234–235) also criticizes Smith for making his descriptions through the lens of a scholar of religion, but that is who Smith was. After all, he was ordained as a priest. As put by Robert Segal (2008b: 23), he can also be seen as a theologian, as "Smith's account of the sacrifice is 'theological' in a straightforward sense: he appeals to God as a cause of evolution." And in another place in the same article, Segal (2008b: 11) writes, "The basic religious divide for Smith is not . . . between Semites and Aryans. It is between primitives and moderns." For Smith, the only way to fully understand religion was to inquire about its origins. And that could only be achieved by studying the most "primitive" forms of religion—as these were all stages that Christianity had to go through in the past. He goes through this process using the comparative method (Segal 2008b: 12). At the same time, as Smith was interested in understanding entire societies, he saw religion as the primary mover in important social (as well as cultural) changes.

Furthermore, most of Smith's (1912b: 491) criticism of Islam in his account of the journey in Hijaz is directly related to slavery—the custom that he found completely unacceptable and indefensible. Slavery is the main topic of the eleventh (and final) letter published in the *Scotsman*. Apart from remarks about "wastefulness of the slave system" (490), Smith distinguishes between slavery as an institution in Arab society (and thus part of their culture) and the slave trade. He first makes some observations about the social position of slaves—the different status that they have in Arab families and among the Bedouin nomads. Then he turns his attention to the issue of the slave trade, noting that some changes were beginning to be implemented—including the new Wâly of Hejâz directing one of his "guard-houses to be built along the coast to prevent the slave traffic" (596). It did not seem to work immediately, but Smith thought that it was a step in the right direction. As he noted in the conclusion of this letter: "It is well to respect the religious freedom of Moslems; but it is too much to suffer this freedom to be used as a cloak for crime" (597).

Just as in other places in his work, Smith makes a clear distinction between religion as essentially human and moral, on the one side, and immoral acts (like the slave trade) that are justified by some religious people, on the other. He was incensed by what he saw as the intentional ignoring of this practice by the local authorities. On the other hand, as a clergyman, he was also interested in introducing the local (Hijaz) population to "Christian books"—and this was something that he did openly (Smith 1912b: 565). Smith mentions Sheikh Ali Qasim ("a liberal-minded man who has seen the world") as the only inhabitant of Jeddah who had a copy of the Bible in Arabic: "He regards it as necessary to the regeneration of Arabia that people should be willing to learn what is useful from any source . . . and . . . he thinks it right to possess the Christian Scriptures" (565). In this way, "Christian Scriptures" were perceived by Smith as something that would help and perhaps accelerate the modernization of local communities.

NOTES

The epigraph is a quotation by Thomas Stevens, in Taylor 1892: iii.

1. To be more precise, there is worldview that Smith had (with all the imperfections and prejudices associated with the time when he lived), and a worldview that Said believed Smith had. The two have nothing in common. From Said's references, it is clear that he barely read Smith—so it is difficult to see what is the actual basis for his criticism.

2. Smith (1912b: 585) described him as "a man of good education and observant habits, who has served in Syria as well as in Yemen, and appears to have made a careful study of the habits of the people over whom he rules."

CHAPTER 4

ANTHROPOLOGY, RELIGION, AND MYTH

• • •

> We cannot draw inferences for religion from the absence of
> an elaborate mythology; the question is whether there are
> not traces, in however crude a form, of the mythological
> point of view. And this question must be answered in the
> affirmative.
>
> —William Robertson Smith, *Lectures on*
> *the Religion of the Semites*

John Ferguson McLennan was one of the most important influences on Smith. The emphasis on kinship should be considered in a historical perspective, because, as put by one of the greatest anthropologists of the last century, "The traditional anthropological preoccupation with kinship was not only underpinned by the conceptualisation of anthropology as a branch of scholarship specialising in the study of society conceived as 'primitive,' but also by its theoretical interest in the description and analysis of particular 'primitive' societies" (Holý 1996: 5). In his most famous work, *Primitive Marriage*, McLennan (1865: 171) claimed that early human societies ("barbaric," as he labeled them) were characterized by highly promiscuous relationships, which he called "communal marriage." This led first to widespread female infanticide, and eventually (as one would expect) to the "shortage" of women—which, in turn, led to the practice of "bride capture" (from neighboring tribes) as a form of mar riage. Smith (1907: 214) refers to McLennan in his *Kinship and Marriage in Early Arabia*: "If captive women were brought into a kin in any considerable numbers, the local group in the second generation would contain representatives not only of the original stock but of all the stocks from which captives had been made." This is where totemism becomes very important:

> By aid of the totem a man knows what persons in each group are united to him by blood-ties and what persons he may not marry. Totemism has religious as well as social aspects, but its primary importance for the student of early society is that it supplied the necessary machinery for working a law of exogamy and enabling a man to fulfil the obligations of kindred in the complicated state of things which has been described. (Smith 1907: 215)

Smith (1912a: 455) follows McLennan's hypothesis "that the ancient nations came through the Totem stage, or . . . that peculiar kind of Fetichism which has its typical representation among the aborigines of America and Australia." Therefore, totem

> is an animal or plant or heavenly body appropriated as a fetch to all persons of a certain stock. These persons believe that they are descended from the totem, who is reverenced as a protector and friend, and whose name they bear. The line of descent is through the mother, who gives her totem to her children. Persons of the same totem are not allowed to marry. (Smith 1912a: 455)

These early societies that McLennan was writing about were also characterized by matrilineality.[1] This is the origin of the institution of marriage. In the beginning, it was established among the exogamous societies only, and among the endogamous (when marriage became possible within the clan) later. McLennan was the first scholar who introduced the terms *exogamy* (marriage outside one's group or clan—as exemplified by "bride capture") and *endogamy* (marriage within one's own group or clan). When explaining the structure of "primitive" societies, McLennan (1865: 122) also mentions *totem*, quoting a letter sent to him by Lewis Henry Morgan, whose ideas on kinship he strongly disagreed with. For McLennan, *totems* were survivals of the original beliefs in plants, animals, and anthropomorphic gods (1868), and *totemism* was an important characteristic of the early kinship groups (1869–1870). It was not only a religion, as noted by Adam Kuper (2016: 6–7), but also a social system:

> Long ago, totemism had been universal. McLennan identified traces of a totemic system in Siberia, Peru, Fiji, and even classical India. The Greeks had their natural spirits. Totemism was also the point of departure of later systems of thought. It planted the seeds not only of religion but also of science. When the names of animals were given to constellations of stars, this was a legacy of totemism but also the first inklings of astronomy. Beliefs about the descent of human beings from animals gave a faint hint of what would become the theory of evolution.

In the same book, McLennan (1865: 8–9) explained what would later become very important for Smith as the "comparative method": "In the sciences of law and society, old means not old in chronology, but in the structure: that is most archaic which lies nearest to the beginning of human progress considered as a development, and that is most modern which is farthest removed from the beginning." He elaborated, "The preface of general history must be compiled from the materials presented by barbarism. Happily, if we may say so, these materials are abundant" (McLennan 1865: 9).

According to Segal (2008b: 12), "The comparative method shows only similarities among phenomena. But the sole way to show differences is to show where similarities cease." The "comparative method" that Smith used was based on the concept of "survivals," made especially popular by Tylor. These "survivals" were traits of the ancient beliefs and social customs that have been preserved in contemporary societies, even though their original function and meaning were lost or forgotten—as McLennan already wrote. Through exploring survivals among the "uncivilized" peoples, Tylor hoped to show both the origin of modern concepts and customs, as well as some pointers for their future development (Bošković 2004). Survivals were "habits, metaphors, customs, and so on that have 'survived' from an earlier stage of culture and which provide clues to both the reconstruction of past states of mind, and the explanation of seemingly inexplicable practices in European civilisation" (Holdsworth 2006). They became "Tylor's primary tool in tracing the progress of one stage of thought to the next" (Holdsworth 2006). The main problem with this method, as nicely summed up three decades ago by Margit Warburg (1989: 45), was "that deciding whether something is a survival or not must be based on a priori suppositions of the direction and character of historical development. As a consequence the method easily leads to tautologies and/or becomes supported by prejudices."

However, the concept of "survivals" is important in order to fully understand Smith's ideas about "primitive thinking" several decades before a particular comparative perspective was formulated by the French philosopher Lucien Lévy-Bruhl (1857–1939). It is not formulated in value terms, but its formulations are becoming more nuanced as societies become more complex. On the one hand, this complexity is reflected in human connection with specific rituals, enabled through the church. This leads to what historian of religions Joachim Wach (1951: 71) refers to as Smith's idea of "corporate individuality." Individual beliefs and actions were fundamentally bound in the communal rituals, and the core of these rituals was a metaphorical understanding of the world (McKinnon 2014). Smith starts from McLennan's considerations that "there was not any beast or bird upon the earth whose shape or image did not shine in the heavens" (quoted in Black and Chrystal 1912b: 457), and then proceeds to looking for analogies, first in Arabia, and then among the Jews. Smith concluded his 1880 paper claiming that "the people of Jehovah" were just as likely to worship a multitude of deities as any of their neighbors at the time, so that there was nothing predetermined for them; in his own words, "It does not appear that Israel was, by its own wisdom, more fit than any other nation to rise above the lowest level of heathenism" (in Black and Chrystal 1912b: 483, footnote omitted).

In his article "Sacrifice," written for the *Encyclopædia Britannica*, Smith (1886: 132) makes a distinction between "natural" and "positive" religions. The former ones ("nature religions of the civilized races of antiquity") are defined as

> [the] religions which had a predominantly joyous character, and in which the relations of man to the gods were not troubled by any habitual and oppressive sense of human guilt, because the divine standard of man's duty corresponded broadly with the accepted standard of civil conduct, and therefore, though the god might be angry with his people for a time, or even irreconcilably wroth with individuals, the idea was hardly conceivable that he could be permanently alienated from the whole circle of his worshippers,— that is, from all who participated in a certain local (tribal or national) cult. (Smith 1886: 134; see also Smith 1914: 285)

On the other hand, what he understood as "positive" religions were the ones of the inhabitants of the ancient Near East, or, as Smith (1914: 1) put it, "Judaism, Christianity and Islam are positive religions" because they "trace their origin to the teaching of the great religious innovators, who spoke as the organs of a divine revelation, and deliberately departed from the traditions of the past." Smith (1892: 281) also saw these religions as "tribal or national," a concept that introduced a very important social component into the study of religion.

Like the great majority of his contemporaries (with the notable exception of Müller and his followers), Smith believed that the best way to study religion was to examine its most primitive form. In the case of the Semitic peoples, this form was preserved in the life and customs of the Bedouin pastoralists, an argument that he already made in his book *Kinship and Marriage in Early Arabia*. His emphasis on the social components of religion led him to postulate that it is the *action* that matters, much more than the *belief*. The ritual, therefore, must come before the myth. As he famously wrote in the second edition of the *Lectures*, myths do not deserve the prominent place that they had in the scholarly studies of his time, as "this mythology was no essential part of ancient religion, for it had no sacred sanction and no binding force on the worshippers" (Smith 2002: 17). Of much more importance was the performance of specific rituals, the practical aspects through which a society established and reiterated its norms and values, therefore

it follows that mythology ought not to take the prominent place that is too often assigned to it in the scientific study of ancient faiths. So far as the myths consist of explanation of ritual, their value is altogether secondary, and it may be affirmed with confidence that in almost every case the myth was derived from the ritual and not the ritual from the myth; for the ritual was fixed and the myth was variable, the ritual was obligatory and faith in the myth was at the discretion of the worshipper. (Smith 2002: 18)

The connection that specific myths had to specific temples, ceremonies, or ethnic groups (what Smith referred to as "tribes") means that myths primarily serve as means for explanation of the rituals, which has important implications for the study of rituals:

As a rule the myth is no explanation of the origin of the ritual to any one who does not believe it to be a narrative of real occurrences, and the boldest mythologist will not believe that. But if it not be true, the myth itself requires to be explained, and every principle of philosophy and common sense demand that the explanation be sought, not in arbitrary allegorical categories, but in the actual facts of ritual or religious custom to which the myth attaches. The conclusion is, that in the study of ancient religions we must begin, not with myth, but with ritual and traditional usage. (Smith 2002: 18)

Smith believed that ritual should be considered before myth not only in order of importance (in contrast to what was claimed in the majority of the studies of his time), but that ritual literally preceded myth in time (Beidelman 1974a: 64). Actions come first, human attempts to explain and rationalize them afterward.[2] This passage can also be understood as a reaction against the generalizations on the lines of the idea of the "primitive science" of the "savages," as expressed by Lang (1884, 1887, 1911). Smith obviously believed that too much attention in the works of his time was being devoted to the beliefs and "stories about gods," at the expense of the rituals. Rituals should form the basis of any serious scholarship on "primitive religion," since they are essentially social in character, and since they reaffirm places and roles of average human beings within their communities (ethnic groups or tribes). What these individuals believed (or did not believe) in was a matter of their personal choice. What they were performing or participating in was not. Therefore, the importance of myths was based on their role in the society—another aspect of his work that became more prominent through the writings of Durkheim (Maryanski 2014; Ptacek 2015). In Smith's work, this has implications for his understanding of ancient Semitic religions, for, as he clearly stated in the second series of the Burnett Lectures, "the maintenance of the communal religion in its integrity depends on the individual actions of every member, the community through its officials merely watching over individuals and seeing that they do not with impunity imperil their neighbours" (quoted in Day 1995: 44).

In the commentary to the third edition of the *Lectures*, Stanley A. Cook (1873–1949)[3] noted that myths "are specifically of *personal* interest, but, in general, they appeal differently to the different types of mind in normal mixed communities" (in Smith 1969: 502). The notion of the "personal interest" is very important here, considering Smith's emphasis on the social components in all religions. Naturally, since the "positive religions" are much more elaborate and "advanced," this social component becomes more prominent in them. Myths might have been more important to the less civilized cultures, but in Judaism, Christianity, and

Islam, they play a secondary role, more as a remnant and a re-minder of the less civilized stages through which even these religions had to pass.

Although Smith's theory of myth and ritual received high praise by some of the leading scholars at the beginning of the twentieth century (such as, for example, Reinach 1911: 437–438), it stood in sharp contrast to the view about the complexity of the material that myths consisted of (Lang 1884, 1911). Andrew Lang (1885: 202) has already profoundly influenced the study of myth with his notion that myths should be studied as some kind of a "primitive science." The idea of the essential difference between different cultures was the fatal blow to the comparative study of myths. There is a degree of similarity necessary for any comparison, and Lang showed that this degree is not present in, for example, ancient Greek and Australian Aboriginal cultures.

The concept of the subordination of myth to ritual was already challenged in some of the articles for another monument of scholarship, the multivolume *Encyclopædia of Religion and Ethics* (Fallaize 1924). Writing in the same *Encyclopædia*, Hartley Burr Alexander (1924: 752) observed that "the meaning does not stop with the notion of act, it is also the attitude." The attitude is influenced by the belief, which is, in its turn, influenced by the faculty, and so on. The explanation of ritual action is extremely complex, and if we attempt to understand myths primarily as something subordinate to rituals, we will not get very far. The implications of Smith's views for the study of totemism have been criticized by Cook (1902),[4] ignored by Frazer (1996), and completely rejected by the disciples of Durkheim, especially Mauss (1950).

Still, and although frequently overlooked, Smith's view of myth and ritual did have an impact on some very important theorists belonging to the myth and ritual school, as I will show in the following chapters. On the other hand, and despite a favorable reception by Durkheim, it did not exercise great influence in the history of religions, sociology of religion, and related disciplines. Anthropology, however, has been a completely different story—especially when it comes to scholars interested in the study of religion and myth. In order to explain his influence, I will first proceed with some more general remarks about the meaning of myth, and then follow with examples of some notable anthropologists who used, and developed in their own theories, Smith's ideas about myth and ritual.

NOTES

The epigraph is from Smith 1969: 49.

1. A similar idea of the "primitive matriarchal society" was proposed several years earlier by the Swiss legal scholar Johann Jakob Bachofen (1815–1887) in his study of the *Muterrecht*, but McLennan came to his conclusions independently. It seems that Bachofen also influenced Jane Ellen Harrison's interest in ancient societies (see Ackerman 2001).

   To complicate matters further, Korotayev (1995: 92) explored a possibility that there might have been some matrilineal societies in the Arabian peninsula—and he concludes that "the answer to the question posed by the title of this paper is 'yes.' This 'yes' is, of course, now much less emphatic than it was little more than a century ago." This would also add some credibility to Smith's (1912b: 586) speculation about the marriage patterns and kinship in Hijaz.

2. A similar view was expressed in the early 1940s by American philosopher Susanne K. Langer (1971: 126ff., here 128), who noted that "it is not at all impossible that *ritual*, solemn and significant, antedates the evolution of language."

   A major influence on her work, German philosopher and cultural theorist Ernst Cassirer (1874–1945) also believed, following the most influential anthropological theories of his time, that ritual comes before myth (cf. Krois 1987: 85–99).

3. Stanley Arthur Cook studied Semitic languages at the University of Cambridge, where he was later University Lecturer in Comparative Religion (1912–1920), and finally Regius Professor of Hebrew (1932–1938). A fellow of the British Academy, Cook was, among his other tasks, one of the editors of *Encyclopaedia Biblica* (1896–1903), joint editor of *Cambridge Ancient History*, and the editor for the Palestine Exploration Fund (1902–1932).

4. S. A. Cook (1902: 447) actually noted that, if Smith were still alive, he would have modified his position.

CHAPTER 5

MYTH, ITS MEANING AND SOME OF ITS EXPLANATIONS

● ● ●

The English word "myth" (as well as the Portuguese and Spanish *mito*, French *mythe*, etc.) comes from the old Greek *muthos* (μυϑος), which has been associated with a variety of meanings and different concepts since antiquity.[1] According to Hofmann (*Etymologisches Wörterbuch Des Griechischen*, Munich, 1949; quoted in Popović 1987: 7), this word originated from the Indo–European root **mau/mou*, and it is closely related to the Lithuanian *mausti* ("to long for something," "to wish something") and the Serbo-Croatian and Slovenian *misao* or Macedonian *misla* ("thought"). According to another theory (Chantraine 1968–1980, vol. 3: 718–719), it is derived from the old Greek onomatopoeic *mu* (μυ), seen, for example, in the verb *mudzo* (μυδζο)—"to murmur," "to complain."

It is widely recognized today that the clear distinction between μυϑος and λογος (originally "word," "reason," or "plan") did not take place until late antiquity (cf. Ramnoux 1990: 1039; Detienne 1990), despite the fact that our modern (everyday) usage could be dated to the initial distinction made by the Ionian philosophers from the sixth century BCE. The word μυϑος is recorded for the first time in Homer's *Iliad* and *Odyssey* (ca. 750–650 BCE), where it has a variety of meanings, although the main meaning seems to be "word" or "speech." However, in the *Odyssey* it also means "a public speech," "excuse," "conversation," "fact," "threat," "reason," and "story" or "tale." This last meaning leaves open the question of whether it is a true or fictional story (Popović 1987: 7). The meanings from the *Iliad* include "order,"[2] "task," "advice," and "intention" or "plan."

Other Greek writers also used μῦθος for "saying" (Aeschylus, *Choephori* 314), "hearsay" (Sophocles, *Aiax* 226), or "report" or "message" (Sophocles, *Trachiniae* 67). After the beginning of Ionian philosophy in the sixth century BCE, μῦθος was used to denote a "fictitious story," something that has been made up (Pindar, *Ol.* I, 29; Plato, *Phaedo* 61b), or "legend" (Herodotus, *Historiæ* II, 45). It is this set of meanings that comes close to the modern (at least dictionary) translations of the word "myth." As German classicist Burkert[3] (1985: 312) puts it, the great change comes with the age of classical Athens in the fifth century BCE: "Myth is left behind. The word *mythos*, obsolete in Attic, is now redefined and devalued as the sort of story that the old poets used to tell and that old women still tell to their children."

It is from this period on that the now famous binary distinction between "real" (or "rational") versus "mythic" takes place, as exemplified in the well-known passage from Plato's *Phaedrus* (229b–230b):

> PHAEDRUS: Tell me, Socrates, is it not from some place along here by the Ilissus that Boreas[4] is said to have carried off Oreithyia?
>
> SOCRATES: Yes, that is the story.
>
> PHAEDRUS: Well, is it from here? The streamlet looks very pretty and pure and clear and fit for girls to play by.
>
> SOCRATES: No, the place is about two or three furlongs farther down, where you cross over to the precinct of Agra; and there is an altar of Boreas somewhere thereabouts.
>
> PHAEDRUS: I have never noticed it. But, for Heaven's sake, Socrates, tell me; do you believe this tale is true?
>
> SOCRATES: If I disbelieved, as the wise men do, I should not be extraordinary; then I might give a rational explanation, that a blast of Boreas, the north wind, pushed her off the neighbouring rocks as she was playing with Pharmacea, and that when she had died in this manner she was said to

have been carried off by Boreas. But I, Phaedrus, think such explanations are very pretty in general, but are the inventions of a very clever and laborious and not altogether enviable man, for no other reason than because after this he must explain the forms of the Centaurs, and then that of the Chimaera, and there presses in upon him a whole crowd of such creatures, Gorgons and Pegas, and multitudes of strange, inconceivable, portentous natures. If anyone disbelieves in these, and with a rustic sort of wisdom, undertakes to explain each in accordance with probability, he will need a great deal of leisure. But I have no leisure for them at all; and the reason, my friend, is this: I am not yet able, as the Delphic inscription has it, to know myself; so it seems to me ridiculous, when I do not yet know that, to investigate irrelevant things. And so I dismiss these matters and accepting the customary belief about them, as I was saying just now, I investigate not these things, but myself, to know whether I am a monster more complicated and more furious than Typhon or a gentler and simpler creature, to whom a divine and quiet lot is given by nature. But, my friend, while we were talking, is not this the tree to which you were leading us?[5]

Of course, one must add that even in this ancient Greek "age of reason," the same author (Plato) uses myths to explain and expand his own philosophical theories—for example, the myth of Prometheus and Epimetheus in the *Protagoras* (320d–322e), or the allegory of the cave in the seventh and the myth of Er in the tenth book of the *Republic*, etc.[6] But the die had been cast, and the new horizons opened.[7] Another good example of these new horizons comes from Herodotus's famous discussion of the flooding of the Nile (*Historiæ* II, 23–25), where he uses deductive reasoning to arrive at what he believes to be the correct answer.

In his study of the ancient Greek attitudes toward myth, French archeologist and historian Paul Veyne (1988: 24) wrote that "in Greece there existed a domain, the supernatural, where everything was to be learned from people who knew. It was com-

posed of events, not abstract truths against which the listener
could oppose his own reason."[8] Veyne (1988: 23) went on to offer another definition, the one that was based on another understanding of myth in antiquity, influential all the way through the
sixth century CE:

> Myth is information. There are informed people who have
> alighted, not on a revelation, but simply on some vague
> information they have chanced upon. If they are poets, it
> will be the Muses, their appointed informants, who will tell
> them what is known and said. For all that, myth is not a rev-
> elation from above, nor is it arcane knowledge. The muse
> only repeats to them what is known—which, like a natural
> resource, is available to all who seek it.

It was only after the advent of a radically different system of
knowledge in the Middle Ages that this Weltanschauung began
to change. But the debates of antiquity are in many ways re-
enacted in modern scholarship. And one of the many paradoxes
of the study of myth is the fact that interest in it peaks in the
twentieth century, the age of great technological discoveries and
the desperate human search for meanings.

A scholar who exerted considerable influence on more contemporary anthropological interpretations of myth was the
Italian philosopher and legal scholar Giovanni Battista (or Giambattista) Vico (1668–1744). Unable to succeed the highly prestigious and very well-paid Chair of Jurisprudence at the University
of Naples, between 1699 and 1741, Vico became instead a professor of rhetoric at this university, and, in 1734, was also appointed
Royal Historiographer by Charles III, the king of Naples and Sicily. Vico retired from the university because of poor health, and
was succeeded by his son, Gennaro.

His best-known work is *Of New Science* (*La scienza nuova*), the
first edition of which was published in 1725, the second (mostly
rewritten) five years later, and the third (considerably revised,
also referred to as "the definitive one") shortly before his death,
in 1744 (Vico 1982). It was a very complex work, which, at the

time when it was published, was read and understood by relatively few people. The book presented the arguments about the rise of science or knowledge (*scienza*), in opposition to Cartesian emphasis on clear and distinct ideas. According to Vico, the Cartesian hypothetic-deductive method rendered phenomena that cannot be expressed logically (and this included not just sense and psychological experience, but also human sciences) as mere illusions. Full knowledge of anything required discovering *how* it came into being. The main characteristic of humans is that they are *social beings*, as "man makes himself the measure of all things" (quoted in Verene 2015: 120). The main purpose of science is to recover the truth, as it comes to us over time through a *sensus communis*, different cultures, customs, and languages, and to remove "the falsehood" it comes with. Unveiling this falsehood leads to "wisdom," which is the "science of making such use of things as their nature dictates."

"Thus our Science," Vico wrote when referring to *poetic wisdom*, "comes to be at once a history of the ideas, the customs, the deeds of mankind. From these three we shall derive the principles of the history of human nature, which we shall show to be the principles of universal history, which principles it seems hitherto to have lacked" (§ 368). When discussing different stages of development of human societies, Vico referred to "ages of gods and heroes," as consequences of creative acts of imagination. Two kinds of wisdom—poetic and intellectual—reflect the dual nature of human beings (sense and intellect). Institutions first arise from the sensory experience. The entire history of humanity can be divided into three periods, corresponding to the "ages" of individual human life. The first one was "infancy," characterized by naive and childish behavior (§ 376). The second one was "adolescence," or the age of youth, marked by enthusiasm and imagination. Finally, the third age is "the age of maturity," typical for adults, who exemplify *the age of reason*. The so-called "primitives" used gestures and symbols, and their development corresponds to the stage that Vico called "infancy." The second phase of development corresponds to the age of ancient Greek and Roman cultures. Homeric gods were the best example of imagination from this period. Finally, in the age of reason, people finally realized that they are all equal. The realization that people ("men," as Vico put it) are equal means that they have the same nature. There exists a divine spark in everyone, guided by Providence (§ 385).

According to Vico, human beings cannot live without religion and myths. Religion is based on eternal truth, as well as on the awareness of the existence of God. Contrary to rationalist authors writing in the era of the Enlightenment, Vico insisted on the so-called *psychological element*, that is, on that which pertains to the very beliefs of men, and this approach only became popular in the sphere of romanticists' explorations an entire century after Vico. On the other hand, of course, people cannot establish their communities, or exist as human beings, without laws and regulations. That is why, according to Vico, and throughout the whole period of the existence of human society, there was a certain evolution of laws, an evolution of regulations and norms, and this evolution, this gradual development, make human societies possible in the first place.

Myths represent reality, as they are a reflection of a particular culture or society (Vico uses the term "nations" to refer to cultures and societies)—but reality is always presented in poetic or symbolic forms. Myths serve as tools that help nations to understand the phases of their own development. In the first stage of the development of mythology, people attribute human characteristics to various natural phenomena (rain, sun, thunder, etc.). Nature thus becomes "humanized." In the second stage, people begin to dominate over nature, as exemplified by the discovery of fire and other inventions that make human lives easier. The third stage brings development of political institutions in different societies. Finally, in the fourth stage, deities are assimilated into the society, and this is, for example, what Homer did in ancient Greece. Myths are different in different cultures (and different nations) because they originated from very diverse social and cultural situations. In order to understand them (and this goes for all the aspects of human intellectual development), one needs to study different cultures.

This type of explanation represents a relatively early attempt at an essentially relativist perspective when trying to interpret the phenomena of the world. Although respected and read, Vico was not widely popular during his lifetime—the style of some of his writings was considered as too hermetic by the general public. However, after his death, and especially following, first, the translation of *The New Science* in German in 1822, and then in French two years later, he influenced many scholars, primarily historians, but also authors such as Herder[9] and Goethe in Germany. He was also very much respected by the founder of positivism and one of the principal figures of early sociology, Auguste Comte (1798–1857).

The word "myth" became established in the English language only after the 1850s. F. Max Müller (1823–1900) wrote of "mythe," and even "meith" was not an uncommon spelling (Müller 1909: 4n). However, Müller was one of the first scholars to attempt a "rational" analysis of myths. In his case, this type of analysis was based on language, and led him to conclude that myths are products of some sort of a "disease of language." Mythology (which for him meant both the body of myths and a "scientific" attempt to explain them) was a product of the primordial sense of awe in the face of the forces and phenomena of nature.[10] "Mythology is inevitable," wrote Müller; "it is natural, it is an inherent necessity of language, if we recognize in language the outward form and manifestation of thought; it is in fact the dark shadow which language throws upon thought, and which can never disappear till language becomes entirely commensurate with thought, which it never will" (quoted in Cassirer 1953: 5).

The criticism of Müller's theory marks the beginning of the anthropological approaches to the study of myth (Lang 1884, 1911). Lang (1885) criticized what he called a "philological approach"—he even refrained from using the term "comparative mythology," using "folklore" instead. Instead of Müller's methodology, Lang (1885: 25–26) advocated a comparative approach combined with evolutionism, writing that "the hypothesis will be that myth, or usage, is common to both races, not because of original community of stock, not because of contact and borrowing, but because the ancestors of the Greeks passed through the savage intellectual condition in which we find Australians." I already noted that Lang was asked to write an entry on "Mythology" for the ninth edition of the *Encyclopædia Britannica* by Smith, and that he quotes Smith approvingly—for example, when discussing the origins of religion (Lang 1898: 284).

Müller was himself quite aware of the limitations of his approach, and limited himself only to the area of his own linguistic expertise (Indo-European languages)—unlike his followers. However, despite his valiant efforts (and his brilliant critique of evolutionism in anthropology), most of Müller's linguistic analogies today seem extremely naive. Although people recognize the connection that exists between some natural phenomena and the names of some deities, no one would today seriously attempt to base an entire theory on these connections (see also the discussion in Burkert 1985).

The philosophical attempts to interpret myth reach their most elaborate level with the works of German philosopher Ernst Cassirer. In his magnum opus, *Philosophy of Symbolic Forms*, Cassirer (1953–1957, vol. 2) considers myth as one of the stages in the process of "humanization" (see also Cassirer 1922). Myth is also considered to be a part of a wider complex of human perception of the world, for "in the boundless multiplicity and variety of mythical images, of religious dogmas, of linguistic forms, of works of art, philosophic thought reveals the unity of a general function by which all these creations are held together" (Cassirer 1944: 71). Myth is an important symbolic form—a crucial element that enabled the development of human cultures. Myth is a reflection of reality, although it is also considered as "the form of primitive thought" (Verene 1966: 554). It is also a "pattern of culture"[11] that one can encounter in all human activities (Cassirer 1953: 44). Writing about the "basic mythical conceptions of mankind," Cassirer (1953: 10) claimed that "the mythical form of conception is not something super-added to certain definite *elements* of empirical existence; instead, the primary 'experience' itself is steeped in the imagery of myth and saturated with its atmosphere. Man lives with *objects* only in so far as he lives with these *forms*; he reveals reality to himself, and himself to reality."

When writing about "symbolic forms" (which are, in different essays and books where he refers to them, language, art, myth, culture, science, technology, and mathematics), Cassirer (1953: 11) also noted that "each of these is a particular way of seeing, and carries within itself its particular and proper source of light." The *expressive* form, which forms the foundation of the myth, gradually, through historical and cultural development, leads to more *representative functions* (German *Darstellungsfunktion*) of thought, and it forms a necessary stage in the dialectical development process. Just like Vico two centuries before him, Cassirer also believed in the sequence of historical epochs, but was much more optimistic about humans' capacities to bring out the best in themselves, and to live an integrated life with their environment.

Cassirer worked exclusively with secondary sources, aided by having at his disposal an impressive ethnographic collection in the library of his close friend and polymath Aby Warburg (1866–1929; Alcocer 2006; see also Krois 1987: 22). His first critical study of myth was published in 1922, during his close association with the Warburg Institute (1922–1925).[12] However, the anthropological data that he had access to have not always been assembled in a critical manner—as becomes apparent to anyone reading his essays on myth today (Cassirer 1922, 1953). Nevertheless, the fact remains that Cassirer clearly recognized the importance of myth, as well as the connection between language and myth (1953), and the importance of language in human understanding (1942, 1946a). He was also instrumental in warning about the political and ideological uses and abuses of myths and rituals, based on the experience of Nazism and World War II (Cassirer 1946b)—something that scholars after him developed further, using different case studies (Kapferer 1988). In this latter aspect (and especially in the posthumously published *The Myth of the State*), he contrasted the consequences of politics governed by mythical ideas with the ones governed by reason (Pedersen 2008).

The psychological approach to the study of myth culminates in the work of American literary scholar Joseph Campbell (1904–1987). Campbell taught at Sarah Lawrence College in Bronxville, New York (between 1934 and 1972), and became famous with his book *Hero with a Thousand Faces*, originally published in 1949. This extraordinary study was to a great extent influenced by the theory of the "birth of the hero," about which Austrian psychoanalyst Otto Rank (1884–1939) already wrote in 1909. Campbell (2004: 35–36) believed that there is a single basic myth (*monomyth*) shared by different cultures all around the world—both in space and in time:

> The composite hero of the monomyth is a personage of exceptional gifts. Frequently he is honored by his society, frequently unrecognized or disdained. . . .
> . . . The godly powers sought and dangerously won are revealed to have been within the heart of the hero all the time. He is "the king's son" who has come to know who he is and therewith has entered into the exercise of his proper power—"God's son," who has learned to know how much that title means. From this point of view the hero is symbolical of that divine creative and redemptive image which is hidden within us all, only waiting to be known and rendered into life.

The "cosmogonic tales" are present in all the world myths, and they bring "joy of a transcendent anonymity regarding itself in all of the self-centered, battling egos that are born and die in time" (Campbell 2004: 42). According to Campbell (2004: 10), "It has always been the prime function of mythology and rite to supply the symbols that carry the human spirit forward, in counteraction to those constant human fantasies that tend to tie it back." His main theoretical contribution is the idea of the four main "functions" of myths. In the third volume of his monumental *The Masks of God*, he describes these four functions (1959–1970, vol. 3: 519–522). The first one is installation of a sense of awe before what Campbell called "the mystery of existence," a feeling that also incorporates the recognition of the concept of the numinous, the divine—something characteristic of all religions. The second basic function is the establishment of a cosmology, or specific image of the universe. The third one is support for the existing social order, since myths are always essentially conservative, and they always tend to support the existing social relations. It also provides a divine justification for various social practices, like the caste system in India (Segal 2015b: 176). Finally, the fourth basic function is introducing individuals to the order of reality of their own psyches, leading them toward their spiritual self-realization. Thus, understanding myths also helps people understand the most intricate mysteries about their existence.

Apart from his heavy reliance on psychological theories (especially the concept of the archetypes, made popular by psychologist/psychoanalyst C. G. Jung [1876–1961]), his emphasis on (and perhaps obsession with) a particular cultural horizon (India) makes it difficult, if not impossible, to generalize. Practically speaking, it is impossible to have an equal (or at least comparable) amount of information about all the cultures of the world—which is what he was trying to achieve.[13] At the same time, Campbell was for several decades, and especially in the United States, "the face of myth"—someone who frequently spoke both in public and in the media about the beauty and value of studying myths and, by extension, about learning about other cultures.[14] This also made him one of the icons of the pop culture of the mid-1960s and early 1970s, and some of the most important movie directors of the late twentieth century (such as George Lucas) claim to have been influenced by him.

Another very influential twentieth-century theory of myth is associated with the impressive oeuvre of the Romanian-born American historian of religions Mircea Eliade (1907–1986). Eliade regarded myths primarily as sacred stories related to the events that occurred *in illo tempore*, in the mythical time following the creation of the world, and long before the advent of history. This time "is always the same," as it "belongs to eternity" (Eliade 1959: 88). This mythical time, which he referred to as *illud tempus*, is separated by an immeasurable gap from our (modern) time, and the only way to approach it is through myths. Rituals represent repetition of archetypal events that took place *in illo tempore*. "From the point of view of primitive spirituality, every beginning is *illud tempus*, and therefore an opening into the Great Time, into eternity" (Eliade 1974: 396). Unlike Campbell, Eliade did not allow his strong background in India (Hindu religion, yoga) to bias his research, as he set out to make his theory universal. On the other hand, in shaping his theory of myth, Eliade was strongly influenced by certain conceptions of the native Australians—particularly regarding the concept of the Dreamtime, the *altjeringa* of the Arunta of western Central Australia.[15] Despite the claim that he was interested in two basic types of understanding myths, ancient and modern, in his work he put strong emphasis only on the former aspect (Masuzawa 1989: 321). This has also led some scholars to conclude that, for Eliade, myth triumphs over history (Widengren 1971: 168). This is in line with his belief that, in the age of rapid succession of technical discoveries and breathtaking scientific innovations, humans have simply "forgotten" the time when they were truly free, the Dreamtime of the Arunta.

The fundamental difficulty with his approach is that, although it stimulates phenomenological understanding of myths[16] (as well as religion; for Eliade, these two concepts are always closely related) from *within* the tradition where they originate and generates some kind of empathic *Einfühlung*, it is hard to see how this theory can be tested less subjectively, and this poses serious obstacles for any serious scholarly research. For, if the gap is immeasurable, why try to measure it at all? If something is unspeakable (by its very nature), why try to speak about it at all?

NOTES

1. This outline of the word "myth" and its etymology is based on Popović 1987.
2. That is to say, "to order someone to do something."
3. Walter Burkert (1931–2015) was the leading twentieth-century scholar of ancient Greek religion. He was very much influenced by the myth and

ritual school (he especially acknowledged his intellectual debt to Jane Ellen Harrison), and developed further some of its insights (Bošković 2006: 77–81). For the criticism of his "myth-ritualistic" interpretations, and especially of his excessive reliance on parallels with biology, see Segal 2000: 262ff.

4. The North Wind.

5. In the original dialogue, in ancient Greek, the measure is "three stadiums," which is equivalent to just under 555 meters. This is the very same passage that F. Max Müller (1909) used to introduce his discussion of comparative mythology, as well as Cassirer (1953: 1–2), to introduce his magisterial essay on language and myth.

6. Cf. Ricœur 1969: 165: "We are encouraged in this attempt [toward dissociating myth and gnosis] by the great example of Plato. Plato inserts myths into his philosophy; he adopts them as myths, in their natural state, so to speak, without trying to disguise them as explanations; they are there in his discourse, full of enigmas; they are there as myths, without any possibility of confusing them with knowledge."

    In his relatively recent article in *The Stanford Encyclopedia of Philosophy*, Romanian classical scholar Catalin Partenie (2014) explains Plato's use of myth as a teaching tool and as a means of persuasion. See also Morgan 2003.

7. For the early views on the nature of myths and their relation to science, an excellent summary is provided by Paul Feyerabend (1981: 1–5, 8–9).

8. This sharply contrasts with O'Flaherty (1988: 25–27), who stated that the opposition between myth and truth actually came from Plato. However, O'Flaherty is definitively not a classical scholar (her main area of expertise is India)—so her observation might have been based on secondary sources.

9. It should be noted that J. G. Herder (1744–1803) was also one of the key figures for the establishment of ethnology in late-eighteenth and early-nineteenth-century Germany, as well as the key figure for the formulation of one of anthropology's main methodological characteristics, what will later become known as *cultural relativism*. Of course, he read Vico in the original.

10. This brief summary of some nonanthropological attempts to explain myth is based on one of my earlier articles (Bošković 1988: 409, which was revised substantially in Bošković 2006). Cohen (1969) and Segal (1980b) both represent excellent examples of studies that take into account more anthropological works. The most comprehensive overview is by Segal (2015a).

11. The original, German, publication was between 1923 and 1929, so this term actually predates the same expression used by Ruth Benedict in

her famous 1934 book. I am not sure that she was aware of Cassirer's work at that time, but this is certainly an interesting case of cross-referencing between philosophy and anthropology.

12. Cassirer was especially influenced by the German ethnologist and historian of religions Konrad Theodor Preuss (1869–1938), who worked in the Berlin Ethnographic Museum. In his writings, Preuss criticized Tylor's ideas about animism, and was very much influenced by Andrew Lang's idea of the "High God," and later also by the French philosopher Lucien Lévy-Bruhl's (1857–1939) concept of "primitive mentality." He conducted extensive field research among the Cora and Huichol Indians in Mexico, as well as among the Uitoto and Kágaba in Colombia. Preuss was very important for promoting German scholars' interest in the study of Amerindian cultures, which gained considerable momentum after World War II.

13. Campbell's ethnic and cultural prejudices also did not help interpreters of his theoretical views. For a very good introduction into Campbell's work, and especially insightful discussion of his antisemitism and other potentially tricky issues, see Segal 1992 and 1997.

14. The PBS TV series, *The Power of Myth*, a series of six conversations with Bill Moyers (2010) broadcasted in 1988, remains one of the most popular programs in the history of American public television. In a recent popular article, Will Linn (2018) claimed that Joseph Campbell influenced a variety of popular movies—from *2001: A Space Odyssey*, through *Star Wars*, and all the way to the latest installment of *Mad Max*. As a matter of fact, parts of the interviews that Moyers conducted with Campbell took place on a George Lucas's ranch.

15. He was also strongly influenced by his own technophobia, but I cannot get into discussion of his personal fears or frustrations here.

16. I am using the term "phenomenological" here in accordance with Husserl's original usage: a model of explanation from the phenomena themselves, essentially trans-subjective. In this sense, it would mean the effort to interpret myths "from the native's point of view" (cf. Geertz 1971). Eliade himself preferred the term "morphology."

In anthropology, the method was first described (without actually using this specific term) by one of the discipline's most important founding fathers, Franz Boas (1858–1942). In his early study of the Iglulik Eskimos, he presented the Iglulik understanding of their world by "using their own words" (Boas 1888).

CHAPTER 6

ANTHROPOLOGICAL APPROACHES TO THE STUDY OF MYTH

• • •

The Cyprian Aphrodite is the Semitic Astarte, and her ritual is throughout marked with a Semitic stamp. It is to Semitic ritual, therefore, that we must look for the origin of the April feast.

—William Robertson Smith, *Religion of the Semites*

William Robertson Smith was the first scholar who tried to formulate the relationship between myth and ritual in terms of what should be considered as primary, and what as a secondary element in the relationship. As already shown in the previous chapters, he clearly gave the preference to ritual. This influenced anthropologists after him to primarily look at the *social* (or sociological) aspects of the cultures and societies they were studying. The myths were considered important primarily because they could tell something about the social organization, kinship, customs, etc. of the societies which anthropologists studied.

The importance of myths was clearly recognized from the beginnings of anthropology as a scientific discipline in the late 1880s. Chapters on "beliefs" and "rituals" were standard in all major ethnographies. A view of the founder of the American anthropology, Franz Boas, was that the native peoples' customs and rituals were rapidly disappearing in light of huge technological advances, rapid industrialization, and enormous colonial expansion. This was leading to the shifts that would bring the permanent disappearance of native cultures all over the world, something that Boas rightly saw as the legacy of all humanity. One way to preserve this legacy in the United States was to go to the field and record Native American histories and narratives, gathering data about their cultures—as many as possible and as quickly as possible.

Of course, now we know that Native American societies (just like many other traditional communities all around the world) were constantly changing and adapting to new and often very difficult and even hostile circumstances, not disappearing, but the misconception of Boas and his disciples led to the production of some excellent collections of narratives and some very valuable ethnographies. In fact, there is probably no time period that can match the amount of ethnographic data published about Native American cultures in the first two decades of the twentieth century. *Tsimshian Mythology* stands as one of the finest examples of scholarship from this period.

In this magnificent volume, Boas attempted to present a summary of the customs and society of Tsimshian Indians from British Columbia. This account, a monumental research report, was actually a collaborative effort. It was based on the stories collected and transcribed in English by a native Tsimshian historian and storyteller, Henry W. Tate (1860–1914)—although Tate and Boas never actually met (Maud 1989). Tate sent the transcribed and translated texts, which Boas then edited and prepared for publication. In his comments and notes about Tsimshian myths, Boas (1916: 31) attempted to make a clear distinction between myths and tales (1916: 31), but without much success, since he realized that for the Tsimshians themselves, there was no difference—at least none that the outside observer could be aware of. In the end, he settled for a compromise, describing the volume as "a series of tales all of which are considered by the Tsimshian as myths" (Boas 1916: 595).

The issue of distinguishing between myths and "ordinary" or "folk" tales has puzzled anthropologists since Andrew Lang. The problem was clearly recognized by scholars that were regarded as functionalists, beginning with Bronislaw Malinowski.[1]

Malinowski's most famous fieldwork experience came partly as an accident (the outbreak of World War I) and partly as a result of his fellow anthropologists urging Australian authorities to allow him to conduct some research—he was officially regarded as an "enemy alien" (as a citizen of the Austro-Hungarian Empire, even though he had already moved to London) after World War I broke out in 1914. He ended up in Kiriwina, one of the Trobriand Islands, off the Northeastern coast of Papua New Guinea, where he conducted research in several intervals between 1915 and 1918 (Young 2004). This experience eventually resulted in three monographs about different aspects of cultures and societies of the Kiriwina Trobriand islanders, the first of which, *Argonauts of the Western Pacific: An Account of Native Enterprise and Adventure in the Archipelagoes of Melanesian New Guinea*, was published in 1922 (Malinowski 1961).[2] Some sections of this monograph deal with the myths and rituals connected with the Kula.[3]

Malinowski believed that myths represent a "pragmatic charter," a set of rules or codes of conduct, that enable the social functions of a culture to flourish. "The *myth* comes into play when rite, ceremony, or a social or moral rule demands justification, warrant of antiquity, reality, and sanctity" (Malinowski 1926: 28). Like Boas before him, Malinowski sought to distinguish between three types of tales that he encountered in the Trobriand Islands. Unlike fairy tales and legends, which are told "for amusement" and as "a social statement" intended to "satisfy social ambition" (Malinowski 1926: 28), myth is "a reality lived" (18), "not symbolic, but a direct expression of its subject-matter; it is not an explanation in satisfaction of a scientific interest, but a narrative resurrection of a primeval reality" (19).

This, of course, stood in sharp contrast to Smith's words, since, for Malinowski, myths offer justification for belief. They are again intimately associated with rituals (on mythology of the Kula, see Malinowski 1961: 299ff.), but in an inverted order of importance. Even if rituals do come first, myths are necessary in order for one to comprehend the meaning and true function of rituals. If rituals form a re-enactment of the events that are considered to have happened in another reality,[4] myths are necessary in order to place individuals (and the society or the culture itself) within that reality.

In the *Argonauts of the Western Pacific*, Malinowski (1961: 304–305) distinguished between several classes of myths. The "oldest myths" describe events that occurred when the earth was being inhabited from the underworlds, and they are related to the origin of the first human beings, clans, and villages, as well as the relationship between this world and any future world. What he called the "kultur myths" relate to ogres and cannibals, as well as to the human beings who established some important customs and ceremonies. They refer to the events in time when human beings already inhabited the earth, and when social customs are already established. Stories about the Trobriand culture hero, Tudava, were also included within this category of myths. Finally, the third class consists of "myths in which figure only ordinary human beings." These human beings do have extraordinary powers (especially the power of magic, which is, for Malinowski, closely related to religion), and these stories describe the origins of witchcraft, love potions, and flying canoes, as well as some Kula myths (Malinowski 1961: 311–316).

Of course, many myths fall within two or even all three of these categories (Malinowski 1961: 305), and the distinctions between these categories are not always clear. The main force that lay behind the life of the Trobriands was "the inertia of custom" (Malinowski 1961: 326). Since the Trobriands paid so much attention to the customs, Malinowski (1961: 327) concluded that "the past is more important than the present." Stories from the past also possess an element of universality (everybody knows them and everybody talks about them), and this contributes to the normative function of myths. Perhaps it is only fitting that his own biographer, Michael Young (2004: 610), concluded his impressive account of the formative years of Malinowski's life (his book covers the time period until 1920) by comparing him to a Trobriand mythical hero, Tokosikuna.

The emphasis on normative and social aspects clearly distinguishes anthropology from other disciplines that deal with myths, like philosophy (Ricœur 1990), history (Ricœur 1987), or history of religions (Boon 1987). Another important distinction is the emphasis of anthropologists and ethnologists since Smith on the ritual action itself. In anthropology and ethnology, this emphasis on ritual action was mostly taken for granted, and myths and rituals were just studied together, without any attempt to clarify their relationship. One of the first scholars that attempted to clarify this relationship was American anthropologist Clyde Kluckhohn (1905–1960).

In his seminal article "Myths and Rituals: A General Theory," originally presented in a lecture in 1939,[5] Kluckhohn (1942: 45–46) elaborated on the "connection between rite and myth," clearly recognized by psychoanalysts such as Reik and Freud, who "verbally agreed to Robertson Smith's proposition that mythology was mainly a description of ritual." This reference to psychoanalytical interpretations is not an accident, since Kluckhohn (1942: 50–52) was very interested in various psychological explanations, which he believed to have been neglected in prior anthropological research. A classicist with a wide range of interests and a lifelong passion for studying the Navahos, Kluckhohn studied anthropology in Vienna in 1931/1932, and there became acquainted with the then-current psychoanalytical theories. This background will be obvious to anyone reading his article—especially in light of the emerging debates about "genuine" and "other" cultures (the most important contribution is Benedict 1934). In his article, Kluckhohn (1942: 46–47) also pointed to the difficulties of making a clear distinction between myths, legends, and fairy tales—unlike Malinowski before him.[6] He did consider a general definition of myth as a "sacred tale" (Kluckhohn 1942: 47),[7] but found it unsatisfactory because of the lack of association with ritual.[8] And, while there certainly were cultures that associated myths with rituals (here Kluckhohn gave an example of the Christian Mass), there were clearly others (and here he drew on his already extensive fieldwork experience among Navahos and Pueblos from the American Southwest) that did not. As a matter of fact, according to Kluckhohn (1942: 54), "the whole question of the primacy of ceremonial or mythology is as meaningless as all the questions of 'the hen or the egg' form."

For Kluckhohn (1942: 54), the truly important thing is the recognition of the "intricate interdependence of myth (which is one form of ideology) with ritual and many other forms of behavior." Here Kluckhohn gave full credit to Malinowski (1926), although he in fact went much further by pointing at the potential absurdity of another "hen or egg" type problem. Together with Boas and Benedict, Kluckhohn opposed any grand generalizations or "simplistic statements." He insisted that there is no practical way to establish the primacy of one or the other; one can look only at the "general tendency" within a specific culture. This tendency will depend on a number of specific cultural traits, as well as on the individual responses to these traits (Kluckhohn 1942: 70). In the end, Kluckhohn (1942: 74) remained close to the psychology-influenced theories, since he concludes that "myths and rituals equally facilitate the adjustment of the individual to his society." They have "a common psychological basis" (78), and in a sense they are both "supra-individual." At the same time, they are both "cultural products, part of the social heredity of a society" (79).

The idea of both myth and ritual as cultural products was further developed by Sir Edmund Leach (1910–1989). Like Malinowski (whose seminars in 1936 inspired Leach's interest in social anthropology), Leach was also caught up during the war (in his case, World War II) in the area where he was doing his fieldwork, Burma (today Myanmar). Several years earlier (in 1938), his initial fieldwork in Kurdistan had also been frustrated by another major political crisis (the Munich declaration), so this almost looked like a pattern. However, Leach was able to reconstruct some of his field notes, and, following some intensive archival work after the war, he was finally able to defend his PhD, and to eventually publish his brilliant monograph on the *Political Systems of Highland Burma* in 1954.

Just like Smith's, Leach's discussion of myth and ritual is rather brief, confined to less than seven pages of the introduction. Unlike most of his famous predecessors, Leach did not attempt to define ritual, and, from his perspective, any particular definition (except one as broad as "a system of symbolic communication" [Aijmer 1987: 7]) would be irrelevant. What is relevant is the very specific context he provides for any situation where rituals are observed. In this approach, Leach attempted to reconcile divergent views represented by Durkheim, Mauss, and Malinowski before him. The solution, in his opinion, was a view of *ritual* as something related to *technique*, just as *sacred* is related to *profane*. They "do not denote types of action but aspects of almost any kind of action." Ritual "is a symbolic statement which 'says' something about the individuals involved in the action" (Leach 1970: 13). This is an interesting statement, especially taking into account how a recent commentator traced Durkheim's (as well as Mauss's and Hubert's) ideas of sacrifice as originating in social life to his reading of Smith (Ptacek 2015: 82).

"Myth, in my terminology," wrote Leach (1970: 13), "is the counterpart of ritual; myth implies ritual, ritual implies myth, they are one and the same." He thus consciously stepped away from what he regarded to be "the classical doctrine in English social anthropology" which, according to him, claimed

> that myth and ritual are conceptually separate entities which perpetuate one another through functional interdependence—the rite is a dramatization of the myth, the myth is the sanction or charter for the rite. . . . As I see it, myth regarded as a statement in words "says" the same thing as ritual regarded as a statement in action. To ask questions about the content of belief which are not contained in the content of ritual is nonsense. (Leach 1970: 13–14)

This presents a radical break with functionalist approaches, and an important step toward structural interpretations of myth.[9] For Leach (1970: 14), myths are only "one way of describing certain types of human behaviour"; furthermore, "ritual action and belief are alike to be understood as forms of symbolic statement about the social order." This is possible because rituals, as observed in their cultural contexts, are always patterns of symbols, and they have the same structure as the other pattern of symbols, consisting of the phrases and technical terms that the anthropologist devises in order to interpret them (Leach 1970: 15).

This structure is "the system of socially approved 'proper' relations between individuals and groups" (Leach 1970: 15). Although this system is not always practically recognized, "if anarchy is to be avoided," members of the society must be reminded of the underlying structure that provides the frame for all of their social activities. "Ritual performances have this function for the participating group as a whole; they momentarily make explicit what is otherwise a fiction" (Leach 1970: 16). In his attempts to interpret rituals in terms of *performance*, Leach was actually repeating what the Semitist Hooke wrote some twenty years earlier—without ever referring to Hooke (cf. Segal 2017: 15–16, 26).

In a later stage of his career, during his experiments with the interpretation of some Biblical myths, Leach (1969: 8) came to regard myths as information, not unlike bits in contemporary information systems. During his interest in the analysis of Biblical myths, Leach seemed to regard most Biblical myths as historical narratives. However, he eventually rejected this view and the structuralist notion of the universal processes in human minds as a kind of "metaphysics." His negative attitude toward grand generalizations places him as one of the important predecessors of the "narrative approach"—among the anthropologists who regarded myths primarily as stories (Urban 1991).

In 1955, the article "The Structural Study of Myth" by French anthropologist Claude Lévi-Strauss (1908–2009) symbolically announced the arrival of structuralist method to the anthropological study of myth. In this extraordinary piece, the French professor argued that we should proceed directly from the apparent contradictions that myths pose (Lévi-Strauss 1963: 208). Approximately at the same time as Leach, but more clearly and much more explicitly, Lévi-Strauss recognized myths as a form of communication. Just like Cassirer before him, Lévi-Strauss insisted on the *reality* of myths. Also like Cassirer, he recognized a clear connection between myths and language (since myths are expressed through language). Along the lines of the great Swiss linguist Ferdinand de Saussure (1857–1913), as well as other scholars inspired by him, such as Trubetzkoy, Jakobson and Hjelmslev,[10] Lévi-Strauss recognized another system of signs that could be interpreted in a way similar to how one interprets language. Since myth, just like language, is made of constitutive units, these units "presuppose the constituent units present in language when analyzed on other levels—namely, phonemes, morphemes, and sememes—but they, nevertheless, differ from the latter in the same way as the latter differ among themselves; they belong to a higher and a more complex order" (Lévi-Strauss 1963: 210–211). Lévi-Strauss (1958) called these units *mythemes*. It is only through the analysis of the relations of different *mythemes* (whose structure remains in the unconscious) that one can understand the meaning of a myth. Understood in this way, we can say that myth, using Saussurean terminology, should serve as a kind of an allochronic device, bridging the gap between the synchronic and the diachronic perspectives.

Lévi-Strauss (1987: 200–201) began teaching Amerindian "mythology" in 1952/1953, and in the outline of his first course, he presented three ways of analyzing a myth: "in terms of the reversible or irreversible character of the sequences present in it," in terms of "the tests of *commutability*," and, finally, "the myth, considered as a *thought ritual*, is submitted to a direction which is in some way natural and emerges from the analysis of ritual considered as an *acted myth*. This third method provides a valuable verification of the results obtained by the other two."

His view of the relationship between myth and ritual is a little bit more elaborated in his lectures for 1954/1955. Unlike his predecessors and contemporaries (especially Leach), Lévi-Strauss (1987: 204) pointed out the fact that in many cases (at this time in his career, he was still working primarily with the Amerindian material, mostly Pueblo and Pawnee), there is no proof of the interrelationship between myth and ritual:

There is no myth underlying the ritual as a whole, and when foundation myths exist, they generally bear on details of the ritual which appear secondary or supernumerary. However, if myth and ritual do not mirror each other, they often reciprocally complete each other, and it is only by comparing them that one can formulate hypotheses on the nature of certain intellectual strategies typical of the culture under consideration.

In a way, this brings us full circle in the consideration of the relationship between myth and ritual. For Lévi-Strauss (as well as for Smith, but for entirely different reasons), this relationship is not a matter of great importance—despite the fact that there are important implications for the understanding of rituals in contemporary scholarship (Peirano 2001). Theoretically speaking, any myth can be re-enacted just by being spoken (narrated or written down). As far as the meaning of the myths and their interpretation is concerned, rituals are irrelevant. This is not the place to deal in detail with all the complexities of Lévi-Strauss's considerations of "mythic thinking"—as it was formulated in the four volumes of his monumental *Mythologiques*. The multiple layers of Lévi-Strauss's interpretation go across time and frequently depend on the metaphors that involve art—both visual (like representations present in masks) and performing (like music). However, it is worth pointing out that it is also developed in contrast to the perceived theories of "primitive mentality" and that examples of mythic thinking provide important models for Lévi-Strauss's development of his humanism and universalism (his long association with UNESCO was just one part of this[11]). But it is important to note that this humanism and universalism provide very important tools for anthropology in the contemporary world. Just as, in the late nineteenth century, William Robertson Smith sought explanations of the human predicament in a rapidly changing world, so did Claude Lévi-Strauss a century later. For Smith, metaphorical thinking provided the key to understanding human actions, while for Lévi-Strauss, the key was cognitive patterns that all of us share and rely on.

Within French anthropological tradition, Jacques Galinier (2004) criticized some of Lévi-Strauss' ideas, but still found his general approach useful in his own study of the Otomís from Northern Mexico. Interestingly enough, and contrary to Lévi-Strauss, Galinier (2004: 663) found that Otomís also gave preference to ritual over myth, with a very important role played by the *performance*.

It can be argued that by taking the structuralist method from Saussurean linguistics, Lévi-Strauss tries to extend the usefulness of this method far beyond the Saussure's original intent. In doing this, he would have to modify significantly the method itself (which he does not do) in order to succeed. Nevertheless, the structuralist insistence on language (Saussurean *langue* and *parole*, von Humboldt's *ergon* and *energia*), as well as on the use of signs and symbols in the explanation of myths, was an important step forward. In more than a century since Smith's death, the world had changed. It was time for anthropologists to try to do the same.

NOTES

The epigraph is from Smith 2002: 470.

1. Of course, I do not claim that Malinowski ever regarded himself or his method as "functionalist." As far as I know, he referred to his own method as "eclectic."

2. *The Sexual Life of Savages in North-Western Melanesia* was published in 1929, and *Coral Gardens and Their Magic*, in 1935.

3. Kula refers to a system of ceremonial exchange (the "Kula ring") among the inhabitants of numerous islands in the region, involving shells and necklaces, which are used in order to enhance one's social status.

4. Which is, nevertheless, as real as the one we live in.

5. Several years before this article, an interesting (although very brief) discussion on the value of the myth and ritual approach was published in the September and November 1936 issues of *Man*. On the one side was the greatest anthropological proponent of this approach, A. M. Hocart. On the other side was the famous classical scholar H. J. Rose, who was much more skeptical about the feasibility of the "myth-ritualistic" study. I believe that Rose's expertise in a specific area (ancient Greece) outweighed Hocart's more general argumentation.

6. A clear impossibility of making this kind of distinction was later demonstrated by Kirk (1974: 31–37) on the material from Greece. Myths from ancient Mesoamerica also combine elements of stories and fairy tales (Bošković 1989, 1992, 2006, 2017).

7. Nevertheless, there is at least one place in the text (Kluckhohn 1942: 59) where he does use this definition himself.

8. In this article, Kluckhohn uses words *ritual*, *rite*, and *ceremony* interchangeably.

9. The works of Lévi-Strauss became better known in the English-speaking world only after 1955. However, Leach read them well before that, and they corresponded for a number of years. In 1965, Leach called the *Elementary Forms of Kinship* "a splendid failure," even though some years earlier he wrote to him, "Your devastating lucidity arouses my envious admiration" (quoted in Loyer 2018: 409).

10. For the practical as well as theoretical aspects of their works, I refer to overviews in Nöth 1990. See also the chapter on myth (almost exclusively dedicated to the structuralist aspects of study) in the same volume (Nöth 1990: 374–377).

11. United Nations Educational, Scientific and Cultural Organization.

CHAPTER 7

MYTH AND RITUAL SCHOOL

● ● ●

There is some reason to think that in early times Adonis was sometimes personated by a living man who died a violent death in the character of the god. Further, there is evidence which goes to show that among the agricultural people of the Eastern Mediterranean, the corn-spirit, by whatever name he was known, was often represented, year by year, by human victims slain on the harvest-field.

—James G. Frazer, *The Golden Bough*

The term "myth and ritual school" usually refers to a number of individual scholars, especially from Great Britain—sometimes referred to as the "Cambridge ritualists," despite the fact that one of their most important members (Marett) was from Oxford—and Scandinavia (also known as the "Uppsala school"), who emphasized the role of the king (as personified god) in the overall cultural patterns (Ackerman 1991, 2007; Harrelson 1987; Hocart 1936; Rose 1936). The most famous example of this kind of scholarship is Frazer's *Golden Bough*—although in terms of both methodology and focus, some of the main representatives of this "school," such as Samuel H. Hooke (1874–1968) and Edwin Oliver James (1888–1972) sought to distance themselves from Frazer—despite the obvious influence that he had on them. The leading contemporary scholar of myth, Robert Segal (1980a: 173), some time ago wrote about the ambivalent relationship between Frazer and representatives of this school of thought—a view that is also reflected in Ackerman's (2007) assessment of their work.

In his presidential address to the Folklore Society, published over four decades ago, J. R. Porter (1977: 136) claimed that, given the complexity of the data, there was a question of how far it would be possible to speak of such a common pattern (of king as personified god) throughout the ancient Near East at all, and whether the very

> term "pattern" could legitimately be used in the sense in which the scholars associated with this school are supposed to have used it. On the other hand, granted that it seems that a pattern of this kind did exist in what may be seen as a recognizable area marked by a distinctive culture, the question is whether the "Myth and Ritual" scholars provided a correct description of it, did it have, or have to have, wherever it appeared, the features which those scholars regarded as essential to their reconstruction of it? . . . The ideas put forward in the volumes by S. H. Hooke . . . , *Myth and Ritual* and *The Labyrinth* were enthusiastically seized upon by other investigators, notably in Scandinavia. Some of these primary ideas were carried much further and developed in ways of which Hooke and James did not wholly approve. As a result, supposed criticisms of the Myth and Ritual school have often been directed against the more extreme views of some of its followers, rather than against the original begetters, and it was just this danger which caused Hooke to be so wary of the label "school" being applied to all those who were influenced by the conclusions of the Myth and Ritual scholars and pursued their basic theses in their own studies.

There is a long history of the appreciation of and reactions to Smith's work by members of the Folklore Society. One of the first (and quite comprehensive) assessments of the *Religion of the Semites* was published in *Folklore* in September 1890, and its author claimed that Smith's book, together with *The Golden Bough*, which was presented in the same article, were "a veritable triumph for folk-lore" (Jacobs 1890: 384). Following the initial praise, Jacobs (1890: 391) criticizes both Smith and Frazer, although Frazer fares a little better, as his "literary skill is to be recognised through-out, both in arrangement and his clear and careful summaries at appropriate pauses of his argument." Smith is criticized mostly for his style ("dogmatic") and because he did not use enough Hebrew materials, while Frazer's theories are dismissed as simply "incongruous" (Jacobs 1890: 391).

William Robertson Smith influenced generations of anthropologists (including Frazer, who dedicated to his major work to him [Ackerman 2008]). Of particular interest to anthropologists was his discussion of the relationship between myth and ritual. As he famously wrote in the second edition of the *Lectures*, and in the passage that I quoted above, "It follows that mythology ought not to take the prominent place that is too often assigned to it in the scientific study of ancient faiths. So far as the myths consist of explanation of ritual, their value is altogether secondary, and it may be affirmed with confidence that in almost every case the myth was derived from the ritual and not the ritual from the myth; for the ritual was fixed and the myth was variable, the ritual was obligatory and faith in the myth was at the discretion of the worshipper." Therefore, it follows "that in the study of ancient religions we must begin, not with myth, but with ritual and traditional usage" (Smith 1914: 17–18).

This particular view was also important in understanding the place that the individuals had within their own societies, as put in one of the press reports from the lectures in 1887:

Every man as a member of the State was held bound to conform to the traditional rites and usages; but, if this were accurately done, according to precedent, he was free to interpret them as he pleased. It was, therefore, false method to begin with mythology in the study of antique religions. To learn what these religions really were to the worshippers, it was to the institutions of religion that attention must first be paid—the myths, so far as they were not mere inventions to explain ritual, were philosophical, political, genetical, but not properly part of religion itself. (Anon., n.d.)

Unlike Tylor, who saw myth as an explanation of the world, Smith viewed myth as an explanation of ritual. For Tylor, myth explains physical events; for Smith, social events. However, myth, for him, only gains importance when a purpose of some ritual had been forgotten. Even its explanation was slightly more than just an account of the origin of a ritual.

This was further developed by some other British "myth-ritualists," such as, for example, the already mentioned Stanley Cook (1969: 500–503), who distinguished between what he called "primary" and "secondary" myths in Smith's work. The "primary" ones were connected with the system of beliefs and the specific worldview, and they were primarily associated with the ritual action. On the other hand, what Cook has called "secondary" ones have been less important. As he put it, "They are based upon misunderstandings (e.g. of images, words, names); they are explanations of explanations, the key to an old tradition having been lost" (Cook 1969: 501). Of course, it would still be possible for these myths to get "purified" and reworked into "pleasing tales," but in all cases these myths are very remote from the concepts associated with them in "primitive" cultures. While accepting the concept of the greater importance of ritual action, Cook (1969: 501) also noted "the risk of going into another extreme and making the distinction between myth and ritual too absolute."

In his overview of "the ritual view of myth," American literary critic Stanley Edgar Hyman (1955: 463) traces a genealogy that connects Tylor and Smith (through the comparative method), but also to Frazer and then Harrison. According to classical scholar and probably the most important representative of the myth-ritualists,[1] Jane Ellen Harrison (1850–1928), "The meaning of myth could never be fully understood purely as an artifact of language ... but instead had to be sought in the behaviour, the lived experience ... of those from whose lives the stories emerged" (quoted in Ackerman 2001: 68). In one of her most famous books, Harrison (1912: 328) wrote, "The primary meaning of myth in religion is just the same as in early literature; it is the spoken correlative of the sacred rite, the thing done; it is to *legomenon* as contrasted with, or rather as related to, to *dromenon*."[2] Several decades later, S. H. Hooke (in Blackman et al. 1933: 3) wrote the following, in the multiauthored volume *Myth and Ritual*: "The myth is the spoken part of the ritual: a description of what is being done. The original myth, inseparable in the first instance from its ritual, embodies in more or less symbolic form the original situation which is seasonably re-enacted in the ritual."

Segal (1980a: 175) summarizes the views of Harrison and Hooke:

> By definition, all myth-ritualists presuppose that a relationship of some kind exists between myth and ritual. They differ only over what the relationship is. For William Robertson Smith, myth is an explanation of ritual and arises after the magical meaning of ritual has been forgotten. For Harrison and Hooke, myth is the script of ritual and arises alongside it: "The primary meaning of myth," says Harrison, "is the spoken correlative of the acted rite, the thing done" (1912: 328). The recitation of the myth is as magically potent as the performance of the ritual: "Together with the ritual," says Hooke, "and as an essential part of it there was always found . . . the recitation of the story whose outlines were enacted in the ritual. This was the myth, and its repetition had equal potency with the performance of the ritual" (1935: v).

On the other hand, British-American historian of religions Theodore H. Gaster (1906–1992) insisted on the fact that both myth and ritual refer to a single phenomenon, and therefore they cannot be separated (as Smith did):

> To speak in terms of practical expression: if a king or headman performs a certain act in order (say) to produce rain or avert pestilence, the corresponding myth will portray that act in terms of something done on a transcendental plane

by immortal suprahuman beings. If, for instance, the king or headman ritually engages and discomfits the demon of overflowing or impounded waters in order practically to ensure the prosperity of the crops during the ensuing year, his action will be presented in the concomitant myth as the defeat of the Dragon by the tribal god (or the weather-god) or by, e.g., "Saint George." (Gaster 1954: 186–187)

Smith's influence could be traced to writings of some other influential Old Testament scholars, such as, for example, in the following outline of the important contributions of the Norwegian Old Testament scholar Sigmund Mowinckel (1884–1965):

In all primitive religions the central experience is connected with certain highly important rites which are performed at certain seasons of the year. Most frequently an annual occasion is chosen for these solemn festivities. The purpose of all primitive worship is recreation, and hence such a festival may be called a Recreation-festival or even (though less happily) a New Year's festival. (Quoted by Kraeling 1928: 134)

In his study of *Psalms*, Mowinckel claims that the ritual (or, as he prefers to call it, *cult*),[3] is the essential component of religion:

It has been said that religion appears in three main aspects, as cult, as myth and as ethos. Or, in other terms, as worship, as doctrine, and as behaviour (morals) . . . cult is a general phenomenon appearing in all religions, even the most "anticultic" Protestant sects and groups. It is indeed an essential and constitutive feature of a religion, that in which the nature and spiritual structure of a religion is most clearly manifested. (Quoted in Ap-Thomas 1966: 319)

Mowinckel (1934, 1955) did not believe that the same rituals were taking place all over the ancient Near East (for example, in the ancient Babylonian ceremonies, the king *was* god), but he was strongly of the opinion that there was sufficient evidence from Jewish tradition and the content of the Psalms to show that at least a parallel ceremony was celebrated in Jerusalem during each New Year and that it included at least (a) a triumphal procession around the temple, (b) a recitation of the story of creation, and (c) the proclamation of Yahweh's renewed dominion over the world (see also Ap-Thomas 1966).

Mowinckel, who was a professor at the University of Oslo, devoted most of his time and energy to the study of Psalms. His very influential view of the central role of the ritual ("cult") can be traced back to Smith, as he was the first scholar to consider the relationship between myth and ritual—especially in relation to the religions of the Semitic peoples. He also exerted considerable influence over some other members of the Uppsala school (Ringgren 1988). But this is also something that cannot be considered separately from the whole issue of the interpretation of Biblical texts.

NOTES

The epigraph is from Frazer 1996: 409.

1. Jane Ellen Harrison became the first research fellow of the Newnham College in Cambridge in 1898. She was a member of the first generation of British women with university education and established herself as one of the most famous scholars of her time. According to Ackerman (1991), Harrison was at the same time the finest representative and the central figure of the myth and ritual school, as her acceptance of both Freud's ideas and Durkheim's theories made her the best and the most prolific scholar of her time.

2. Greek terms: *legomenon* means "something said only once," and *dromenon*, "things done."

3. In his writings, Mowinckel used the terms "cult" and "ritual" as synonyms.

CHAPTER 8

METHODOLOGY AND LITERARY CRITICISM

● ● ●

It is a favourite speculation that the Hebrews or the Semites in general have a natural capacity for spiritual religion. . . . That was not the opinion of the prophets, who always deal with their nation as one peculiarly inaccessible to spiritual truths and possessing no natural merit which could form the ground of its choice as the people of Jehovah.
—From *Lectures & Essays of William Robertson Smith*

In order to fully appreciate the circumstances of the origins and development of Smith's theories, it is important to understand the social and cultural background of his writing, as well as the debates about the approach to the scriptures that were going on at the time—both in the United Kingdom (including Scotland) and in continental Europe. Since 1872, he had socialized with other young scholars as a member of the Old Testament Revision Committee, which met regularly in London until 1884 (Booth 1999). Smith came to Biblical studies as part of a generation of young scholars who realized that the ancient scriptures should not (and cannot) be interpreted literally. As the world was rapidly changing (especially during the nineteenth century), new interpretations were needed. This attitude had major implications (Livingstone 2004a). When he published the *Encyclopædia Britannica* entry "Bible," Smith (1875) already firmly posited that even the Holy Scriptures were first and foremost literary *texts*, and that they should therefore be interpreted primarily as *texts*, written by human hand. This was the approach that was also called "literary" Biblical criticism, and by the time of his writing it was already well established in continental Europe, especially in Germany. Since 1867, Smith had spent some time at the universities in Bonn and Göttingen, and was certainly well aware of all the key theoretical developments among Biblical scholars, especially following the seminal work of Einhhorn.[1] At the same time, his efforts should be seen in opposition to a rising tide of general skepticism that arose as a result of the dynamic technological development of the nineteenth century—as well as the introduction of new theories, such as the ones promoted by Charles Darwin (1809–1882) and Alfred Russel Wallace (1823–1913)—but especially Darwin's hypothesis of common descent and his ideas about natural selection. In his public lectures, as well as in his work in the Free Church College, Smith was very actively promoting ideas that were influenced by Darwin's (and Wallace's) theories—something that further alienated him from his more conservative peers (Livingstone 2004a). Furthermore, with his strong beliefs that certain moral values and principles must be the guiding principles for knowledge, he might have ignored some aspects of everyday life, as noted by Douglas (1995: 292): "If Smith had been more sensitive to political tensions in the Free Church he might have moderated the too forthright expression of his views." Bailey (1973: 287), one of the best commentators of Smith's theological work, provides a wider context for understanding different developments in his methodology:

Robertson Smith was trained by A. B. Davidson . . . and Albrecht Ritschl . . . . Greatly influenced by the writings of Richard Rothe (1799–1867) and the Reformers, he was an opponent toward science's claim to disabuse people of their need for religion. He showed similar dissatisfaction toward Reformed scholastic dogmatics. From his reading of Rothe he adopted an epistemology which held that the deepest ranges of understanding were attainable through interpersonal fellowship.

Bailey then points to the fact that "in his inaugural lecture of 1870, Smith interpreted Luther and Calvin by means of this epistemology, and he emphasized their recovery of the category of the Word of God as the medium for interpersonal fellowship between God and man." Therefore, it follows that

> the Reformers gave Smith great encouragement by their holding to the principle of higher criticism and their elementary use of it. Through this methodology readers of the Bible could stand in the same position as the biblical characters in order to hear God's address as it had been spoken definitively. Only then could the Holy Spirit effect a response in faith by which the reader moved into the objective word of the text for fellowship with God. Smith prized Calvin in that he went on to project a biblical theology which would integrate exegesis into a sweeping history of God's dealings with man from the fall of man to the resurrection of Christ. Ritschl, after reading his inaugural lecture, alerted Smith to the fact that God's address was spoken in the context of human need which higher criticism could describe, and this completed the essentials of his theological undergirding of higher criticism. (Bailey 1973: 287–288; footnotes omitted)

In the essay about Smith's 1881 book *The Old Testament in the Jewish Church*, J. W. Rogerson (1995: 176) wrote that "Smith was an enthusiast for biblical criticism because he believed that it freed the Old Testament from fetters that made it a closed book . . . . With the help of criticism . . . the Old Testament could be used to write a history of grace, recording God's successive acts of grace to his people adapted to the quite different situations of an unfolding history."

All of this clearly casts Smith as one of the representatives of the approach that was already established in Europe.[2] Moreover, the whole idea of the "literary approach" as one of the aspects of "Biblical criticism" was quickly adopted by a number of scholars in Northern Europe in the early twentieth century. Among them, the most prominent were the Swedes Henryk Nyberg (1889–

1974), Ivan Engnell (1906–1964), and Geo Widengren (1907–1996), as well as the Danes Vilhelm Grønbech (1873–1948) and Johannes Pedersen (1883–1977). Additionally, one of the most important scholars for the establishment of contemporary Biblical studies, Yehzekel Kaufmann, in his article "The Bible and Mythological Polytheism" (1951), specifically referred to important contributions of the representatives of the "Scandinavian school," noting that their research presented important aspects that needed to be considered in Biblical interpretation.

Nyberg, an Orientalist who believed that the Iranian influence was essential for understanding ancient Biblical (as well as Middle Eastern) texts, thought that the oral tradition had to be

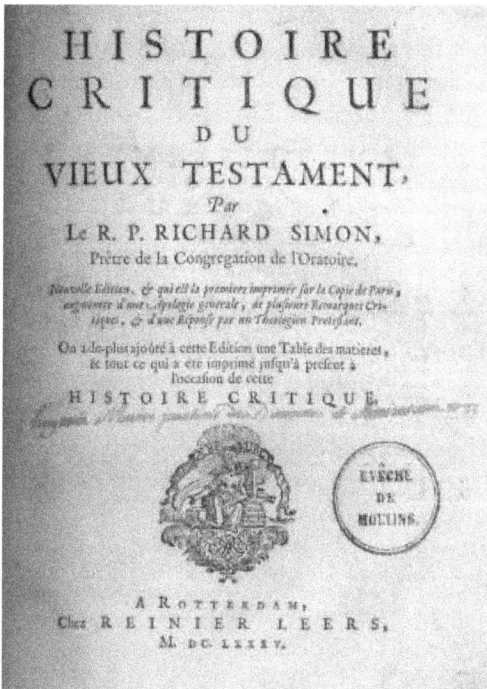

Figure 8.1. Title page of Richard Simon's *Histoire critique de vieux Testament* (1685 edition), which established critical study of the Bible. Work in the public domain.

taken into account when interpreting ancient texts. In this, he followed the tradition of "Biblical criticism" as it was established by the mid-nineteenth century. This type of approach was not considered very unusual or radical in Scandinavia. Through insistence on the importance of oral tradition, Nyberg also influenced his student Widengren (who would later become a major figure in the study of comparative religion),[3] who, in turn, influenced Engnell, especially the ideas that he would publish in his seminal *Studies in Divine Kingship in the Ancient Near East* in 1943 (Engnell 1967).[4] This is an example of a very interesting scholarly genealogy—but it could hardly be imagined without Smith's ideas.

The extent of the influence of the myth and ritual school on Engnell was something that was obvious to scholars writing about him or referring to his works (Ahlström 1965: 337). Among other things, he wrote that "the ancient Near East . . . is characterized by a more or less homogenous cultural level dominated by the institution and ideology of the sacral kingship" (Engnell 1998: 138). In his study of the New Year festivals of ancient Israel, Engnell focuses on the king's reinstallment ("Enthronement") and the renewal of vegetation—somewhat less dramatic than Frazer's insistence on the slaying of the god/king, and the physical death and rebirth of vegetation. This makes the king "*ideologically* divine" (Ahlström 1965: 337, emphasis in the original). Furthermore, Engnell connects these rituals with the similar ones in other ancient Mesopotamian cities (Uruk, Ur), as well as with the patterns preserved in rituals such as the ones in the Babylonian epics *Enuma eliš*, or *Akîtu*.[5] In order to trace these influences, it was necessary to critically re-examine the Old Testament psalm material (Engnell 1998: 139–140), and to look for the sources, especially influences "by Eastern religions in the pre-Israelite period" (140).

According to British theologian G. W. Anderson (1950), a particular type of use of oral tradition is of importance when understanding the work of Engnell (whom he singles out as perhaps the best representative of what he refers to as the "Uppsala school").[6] He points to Engnell's emphasis on oral tradition, and insists that, from this perspective, an important part of the work that has to do with the analysis of the Old Testament "must be undone, because it has been carried out in complete disregard of the importance of a reliable oral tradition in the formation of the Old Testament, as of other oriental literatures" (Anderson 1950: 240–241). Anderson (1950: 241) believes that this type of interpretation has its roots in Nyberg's idea that the Hebrew text of the Old Testament was completely "dependent on an oral tradition which was thoroughly trustworthy, and which was the chief means of the preservation of saga, legend, law, and prophecy in the period before the Exile."

> Transmission was not mechanical repetition; but the material was adapted and expanded through succeeding generations. Thus, speaking broadly, in place of the fumbling officiousness of the interpolator[,] Nyberg presupposes the organic growth of a living tradition. Because he does presuppose this development, he has to warn us that we can never be sure of getting back to the *ipsissima verba* of the great personalities of the Old Testament. We must content ourselves with accepting the tradition about what they said. (Anderson 1950: 241; emphasis in the original)

It should be noted that Engnell's insistence on the importance of oral tradition also led him to reject some, as he called them, "western theories," which, he believed, gave too much prominence to literary criticism.[7] Nyberg seems to have believed that the transmission through memorization was a stable and relatively fixed way to transmit ancient texts. Engnell accepted the idea that the Old Testament was essentially an oral tradition, which only later acquired its written form. Anderson also noted that this view was further elaborated by Harris Birkeland (1904–1961), Norwegian theologian and a former student of Mowinckel.[8] Birkeland wrote that the sacred texts were most likely known by the religious specialists, and quoted by heart when it was appropriate. Anderson (1950: 241–242) summarized:

Even where sacred truth is enshrined in canonical scripture, oral tradition continues (an argument which, we may note in passing, cuts both ways, since the existence of a vigorous oral tradition does not necessarily preclude, but may presuppose, the existence of a written text). Birkeland also refers, as Nyberg had not done, to the oral transmission in Islam of traditions which received fixed forms, and to the alleged oral transmission of Arabic poetry before the time of the Umayyads. A similar process of oral tradition, he contends, preserved the material contained in our prophetical books, and arranged it in complexes, so that all that remained to be done when the material was committed to writing was the arranging of the complexes in order.

Danish philologist Johannes Pedersen (1883–1977) was especially influenced by Smith's insistence on what he called "literary criticism." He was much more radical in his approach than, for example, Smith's friend Julius Wellhausen. A fellow Dane, W. Grønbech, the author of the monumental *Culture of the Teutons* (first published in Danish between 1909 and 1912), argued that a "people" could be defined by a specific culture, which could be reduced to a single unifying concept or idea that is present through all the group's ("people's") institutions. Smith (1875: 634) already alluded to this (as well as the relation of God to his people) in the *Encyclopædia Britannica* entry "Bible"—but I will discuss this more in the next chapter. On another level, this can easily be related to what Smith (1902: 17) referred to as studying religion (and its sources) by using "ordinary methods of historical investigation." Pedersen picks this up for the study of the Old Testament. And in the first volume of his monumental *Israel: Its Life and Culture* (1991 [1926]) he takes the concept of the "soul" to be the organizing motif of the ancient Israelite culture. According to him, in the Book of Genesis, "soul" always refers to a "person." Perhaps Smith's idea of the role of Arabic also influenced Pedersen's focus on the structure of Hebrew language (as the key for interpreting aspects of ancient Israelite culture).

On the other hand, the role of beliefs and the role of specific nations, along with Pedersen's idea that the full social context is crucial for interpreting any texts, as well as the general idea about the relationship between peoples and their gods, are all important aspects that were influenced by Smith's studies of Semitic religions. These social aspects had a major influence not only in the study of religion (both comparative religion and history of religions), but also in anthropology and sociology.

NOTES

The epigraph is from Black and Chrystal 1912b: 482–483.

1. Johann Gottfried Einhhorn (1752–1827) was a Biblical scholar and an Orientalist who taught at Göttingen. Following up on the work of the French priest Richard Simon (1638–1712; who published his *Histoire critique de Vieux Testament* in 1682), Einhhorn was one of the first theologians to compare Biblical texts to other Semitic writings.

2. I should add that Bediako (1997: 116) criticizes Bailey for not taking into account all the influences on young Smith's theological views—presenting him as a more independent thinker than he, in her opinion, actually was.

3. Geo Widengren was a philologist and historian, who also studied ethnology as a young man. He was a professor of history and psychology of religion at the University of Uppsala between 1940 and 1973. Between 1960 and 1970, he was the president of the International Association for the Study of History of Religion. Noted for the breadth of his knowledge and his great intellectual curiosity, Widengren was an expert in Iranian, Mesopotamian, and Semitic religions, but he also published studies about Gnosticism, Manichaeism, and Mandaism. Widengren was one of the first historians of religions who elaborated on, and used, the phenomenological method (his *Phenomenology of Religion* was written in 1966; see also Widengren 1971), independently of the Dutch historian and theologian Gerardus van der Leeuw (1890–1950). He already proved the inadequacies of using evolutionism in the study of religion (using the example of J. G. Frazer) in the 1945 article published in *Ethnos*.

4. Of course, and as already noted by Segal (1998: 136), the exact source of the influence was Frazer, via Hooke. However, both Engnell and Hooke sought to distance themselves from Frazer.

5. *Enuma eliš* was the ancient Babylonian creation myth, which referred to the events from the creation of the world, from the time of the Abzu and Tiamat to the enthronement of Marduk as "king of the gods." *Akîtu* was a spring festival, originally probably closely related to agriculture (as the name is derived from the Sumerian word for "barley"), but over time also came to symbolize Marduk's victory over Tiamat (for a condensed discussion of ancient Mesopotamian deities and myths, see the relevant entries by E. K. Glazer, in Bošković et al. 2015).

6. Rev. George Wishart Anderson (1913–2002) was from 1962 professor of Old Testament literature and theology, and from 1968 professor of Hebrew and Old Testament studies, at the University of Edinburgh. I should note that he begins his discussion by explaining that there are "certain problems" when it comes to using the term "school"—as well as in selecting a particular place (in this case, the oldest Swedish university, Uppsala) for its origin (Anderson 1950: 239).

7. This was most likely directed against Mowinckel.

8. Birkeland, who was from 1948 professor of Semitic languages at the University of Oslo, used the structural method in the study of ancient Near Eastern texts. He was regarded as Mowinckel's "favorite student" (Sœbø 1998: 29). Birkeland was already in his 1938 book trying to explore the interplay between the oral and the written, and to slightly move toward interpretation of the written texts. His scholarly interest gradually shifted from the study of Old Testament to the study and interpretation of Qur'anic texts.

CHAPTER 9

SOCIOLOGICAL ASPECTS OF OLD TESTAMENT RELIGION

● ● ●

In its pre-Christian stage the religion of revelation is represented as a *covenant* between the spiritual God and his chosen people the Hebrews.

—William Robertson Smith, "Bible,"
Encyclopædia Britannica

According to William Johnstone (1995), for W. R. Smith, Arabic was of the essence in undertaking "his scientific proof of the divine character of the Old Testament Scripture" (T. M. Lindsay 1894, quoted in Johnstone 1995: 390). According to Johnstone (1995), even his studies of Hebrew rites and ceremonies must be seen through an "Arabic-sensitized" perspective. Therefore, it was very important to study Arabic, if one was to fully understand the earliest scriptures (Burkitt 1894: 687).

The topic of Smith's Burnett Lectures (1888–1891) was described as "the primitive religions of the Semitic peoples viewed in relation to other ancient religions and to the spiritual religion of the Old Testament and Christianity." It is clear that, in this, Smith accepted the evolutionist perspective that was dominant at the end of the nineteenth century (but for some of the important exceptions, see Segal 2001: 346–347).

The god, it would appear, was frequently thought of as the physical progenitor or first father of his people.[1] At any rate, the god and his worshippers formed a natural unity, which was also bound up with the land they occupied. . . . The dissolution of the nation destroys the national religion, and dethrones the national deity. *The god can no more exist without his people than the nation without its god.*[2] (Smith 1892: 281, emphasis mine)

The supreme deity is associated with the concept of the ruler or king (Smith 1886: 133).[3] The local god is in this perspective seen as a mediator between the people and the various aspects of their environment ("nature"), so the worshippers are in a permanent alliance with selected aspects of a natural life (Smith 1914: 124). This is the consequence of religion being "not an arbitrary relation of the individual man to a supernatural power," but "a relation of all the members of the community to a power that has the good of the community at heart, and protects its laws and moral order" (Smith 2002: 55).

According to Engnell (writing in the *Swedish Bible Dictionary*), whose views are summarized by Anderson (1950: 251, notes omitted):

The king is regarded as the son of the deity, and, at the same time, embodies in himself the entire community. He is responsible for victory, success, and prosperity; and he fulfills this responsibility, above all, in the annual festival, in which he appears in a double role. On the one hand he is the suffering Servant of Yahweh, atoning for the sins of the people, and, on the other, the victorious king overthrowing the powers of chaos in the ritual drama which led up to the ceremony of enthronement.

The supreme deity in ancient Near Eastern religions is associated with the concept of the ruler or king (Smith 1886: 133). Again, as put by Smith (2002: 72) in *Religion of the Semites*, "The kingship . . . is not a principle of absolute order and justice, but it is a principle of higher order and more impartial justice than can be realized where there is no other law than the obligation of blood."

The local god is in this perspective seen as a mediator between the people and the various aspects of their environment ("nature"), so the worshippers are in a permanent alliance with selected aspects of a natural life (Smith 1914: 124). "Broadly speaking, the land of a god corresponds with the land of his worshippers; Canaan is Jehovah's land as Israel is Jehovah's people," in the same way as "the land of Assyria (Asshur) has its name from the god Asshur" (Smith 1914: 92).

> We are so accustomed to think of religion as a thing between individual men and God that we can hardly enter into the idea of a religion in which a whole nation in its national organisation appears as the religious unit,—in which we have to deal not with the faith and obedience of individual persons, but with the faith and obedience of a nation as expressed in the functions of national life. (Smith 1902: 20)

The idea of religion as a collective institution and the symbolism related to it is also developed in Theodor Gaster's article from *Numen*:

> The true nature of the relationship between the king and the tribal god is that they are two aspects of the same phenomenon, viewed respectively from the standpoint of the real and of the ideal. The king personifies or epitomizes the "spirit" or character of a living community, as it exists in a particular moment of time. The tribal god, on the other hand, personifies or epitomizes the "essence" of that community conceived as an ideal, transcendental entity of which the living generation is but the present phase. To put the matter in contemporary terms: the king would be the reigning sovereign of Great Britain, while the tribal god would be "the Crown" (or, possibly, John Bull). *Mutatis mutandis*, the relationship is of the same order as that of God the Son to God the Father in normative Christian theology. (Gaster 1954: 188)

Several years later, Widengren (1957) also emphasized the role of the king in ancient Israel as "the mediator"—providing him with a specific role in everyday matters. This is also present in other religious traditions, and Smith frequently referred to examples from ancient Greece in his lectures, stating that "Greek polytheism was not merely a belief in the existence of many gods, but involved the actual worship of many gods and by every citizen" (Day 1995: 62).

This social concept of religion, as developed first by Smith, predates Durkheim and, as a matter of fact, Durkheim (1968: 61, 109n, 455; see also Beidelman 1974: 58 and Rogerson 1979: 231) was quite clear in giving Smith the credit that he deserves.[4] According to Segal (2008b: 23–24),

> Smith is rightly viewed as a pioneering sociologist of religion. He shifts focus of the study of primitive and ancient religion from beliefs to institutions and from the individual to the group. For Smith, the function of primitive and ancient religion is the preservation of the group, even if he does not, like the more relentlessly sociological Durkheim, make group experience the *origin* of religion or make the group itself the *object* of worship.

This is important to take into consideration in his discussion of the development of religious ideas, and arguments for the primacy of new religion, as the new God is a universal one:

> In them [Hebrew stories] God communes with men without ever lowering himself to the level of man. He had no human passions or affections, for his love to his chosen people was raised far above the weaknesses of human preferences. Above all, he was the God of the world before he was Israel's God, while in all the Semitic legends the Demiurge himself was always, and above all, the local king. (Day 1995: 112)

NOTES

The epigraph is from Smith 1875: 634.

1. On the concept of the deity as father ("progenitor and lord"), see Smith 1886: 135.

2. Also Smith 1912a: 463: "There is nothing surprising in the conception that the worshippers are sons of their god." On the "kinship between gods and men," see also Smith 1914: 87–88. Smith (1914: 91ff.) also attempts to explain the concept of the holy, making the distinction between the *sacred* and the *profane*. Like many other aspects of his work, this distinction came into the anthropology via Durkheim.

3. This closely corresponds to information that has been gained from subsequent research into the extensive written records of the ancient Near Eastern cities, since it seems that all of them had a principal deity, who was paired with a consort (Pritchard 1991: 68). The ancient Greek texts, beginning with the *Iliad* and *Odyssey*, indicate the same pattern.

4. This idea was later developed further by Durkheim, in his *Elementary Forms of Religious Life*. "Émile Durkheim indicated that he owed Smith his insights regarding the close relation between people's perceptions of nature and their experience in society, his views on the periodic need for ritual to reinforce social beliefs and values, and his method of explaining religion in terms of the irreducible elements exhibited in its most primitive state" (Beidelman 1987: 366). Segal (2008a: 2; 2008b: 9) also quotes Malinowski's praise for Smith's work: "Robertson Smith [was] the first modern anthropologist to establish the sociological point of view in the treatment of religion."

CONCLUSION

• • •

> The one point that comes out clear and strong is that the fundamental idea of ancient sacrifice is sacramental communion, and that all atoning rites are ultimately regarded as owing their efficacy to a communication of divine life to the worshippers, and to the establishment or confirmation of a living bond between them and their god.
> —William Robertson Smith, *Religion of the Semites*

This journey through anthropology and the history of ideas should open the space for assessments and evaluations of anthropology's rich (and frequently overlooked) history. In the 2012 Marett Lecture, Kuper (2016: 5) claims that "the anthropology of religion was from the first very largely an anthropology of the Bible, with comparative notes from all over the primitive world." Foundations of social anthropology in the second half of the nineteenth century, with the initial studies of kinship and attempts to explain new concepts like totemism, cannot be properly understood without the contributions of William Robertson Smith.

Of course, Smith did not reach his conclusions in isolation. When it comes to some key anthropological topics, his theoretical insights were informed by several of his contemporaries, some of whom became lifelong friends. Perhaps this is nicely illustrated by the following genealogy, which Peter Rivière (1995: 293) used to begin his presentation at the William Robertson Smith Congress:

In 1954, Raymond Firth wrote the Foreword to Edmund Leach's *Political Systems of Highland Burma* and Leach duly acknowledged that Firth taught him most of what he knew about anthropology; in 1936, Malinowski wrote the Foreword to Firth's *We, the Tikopia* and Firth in turn acknowledged a similar debt to Malinowski; in 1922 Malinowski had dedicated *Argonauts of the Western Pacific* to Frazer; Frazer, in 1890, had dedicated *The Golden Bough* to William [Robertson] Smith; and Robertson Smith was quite explicit that the source of his inspiration for *Kinship and marriage in early Arabia* was John Ferguson McLennan.

McLennan's influence can be seen in the observations about polyandry in early Arabia. Smith believed that Arabian societies were matriarchal, and that the turn to patriarchy happened relatively recently, with the advent of Islam. Therefore, when mentioning the status of women, Smith (1912b: 577) notes, "I ought to premise that this is a topic on which it is not easy to get trustworthy information, as customs that appear irregular or contrary to the Koran are not willingly reported." McLennan's "sociological method" was an important source of inspiration for Smith, and it led Durkheim to "discover" Smith in 1895 (Wheeler-Barclay 1993: 59; Rosati 2008: 244). Then it "leads from Durkheim through Radcliffe-Brown to Evans-Pritchard, and so into one of the mainstreams of British social anthropological thought" (Rivière 1995: 301).

Another important area for Smith, both personally and professionally, was religion (Black and Chrystal 1912a, 1912b; Maier 2009; Settembrini 2015). His critical approach is well described in the following lines of the preface that he wrote for Wellhausen's book:

Historical criticism is a comparatively modern science, and in its application to this, as to other histories, it has made many false and uncertain steps. But in this, as in other sciences, when the truth has been reached it can generally be presented in a comparatively simple form, and the main positions can be justified even to the general reader by methods much less complicated, and much more lucid, than those originally followed by the investigators themselves. (Smith in Wellhausen 1973: ix)

The study of ancient Semitic religions offered the way to inquire not just into the origins of rituals, but also into the development of modern societies, as Smith (1914: 2) put in his most famous book: "No positive religion that has moved men has been able to start with a *tabula rasa*, and express itself as if religion were beginning for the first time; in form, if not in substance, the new system must be in contact all along the line with the older ideas and practices which it finds in possession," so the conclusion is that in order "to comprehend a system of positive religion thoroughly, to understand it in its historical origin and form as well as in its abstract principles, we must know the traditional religion that preceded it."

While belief is crucial in the contemporary religion, it was not so in the past; therefore, to understand ancient religions, Smith turns his attention to myth. "Our modern habit is to look at religion from the side of belief rather than of practice," wrote Smith (2002: 16), but "practice" is more important, and it is transmitted through rites, ceremonies, and "rules of ritual." These cannot be studied separately from the myths that accompanied these rites or ceremonies. The explanations of the myth, understanding of what was performed and why—these were the key questions (Smith 1914: 17). He turned his attention to the relationship between myths and rituals, noting that, in his view, rituals are far more important, so "in the study of ancient religions we must begin, not with myth, but with ritual and traditional usage" (Smith 2002: 18). Therefore, he was referred to as someone who "pioneered the myth-ritualist theory" (Segal 1999: 37; 2004: 61). Part of this influence stems from Smith's association, friendship, and influence on Frazer—as a matter of fact, many scholars came to his theories through the lens of Frazer, even though Frazer was very clear (especially after 1910) in stating the differences between their opinions. Smith's influence goes in several different directions: there are British myth-ritualists, led by Harrison and Hooke, who actually position themselves in relation to Frazer (Harrison praises him as her teacher; Hooke "lambasts him as arch-Tylorean"—Segal 1999: 41), there are Scandinavian myth-ritualists (who take the ideas of Biblical literary criticism and develop them further in explanation of, for example, the ancient Israelite society), and there is the relationship between myth and ritual in anthropology. Among the Scandinavian scholars, it is especially interesting to follow the direction in which Grønbech and Pedersen explain the origin and functioning of national institutions, including concept of the "soul" as referred to in Genesis. Smith's emphasis on the kinship between deities and human beings ("a man was born into a fixed relation to certain gods as surely as he was born into relation to his fellow-men"— Smith 2002: 30) influenced scholars such as Gaster in his exploration of the presence of religious symbolism in everyday life (for example, when he described how an important act by a king or headman would be transformed into a myth—as quoted above).

Given the scope of this book, I devoted more space to the influences relevant to anthropology, following a specific genealogy of scholars who had diverging views on the distinction between myth and ritual. (I thought that it would also serve the purpose of this discussion to provide a brief overview of some important and influential theories of myth.) The line of anthropological research that I have explored here starts from Boas, continues via Malinowski (who really appreciated Smith), and then through Kluckhohn, Leach, and Lévi-Strauss. All of them, except Leach, gave preference to myth. Although Smith's general considerations about kinship, together with most of the latter-nineteenth-century theorizing on the topic, have been long rejected (as well as the whole idea of "primitive matriarchy" and shifting kinship patterns in the Arabian peninsula), Smith's influence on the studies of myth and ritual, as well as on the anthropology of religion in general, seems alive and well (cf. Kuper 2016).

I believe that this discussion points to the important influence that Smith exercised in several aspects and on different scholars,

Figure 10.1. Commemorative plaque in Alford Place, central Aberdeen, at former Free Church College. Photo © Aleksandar Bošković.

and that it is important to pay more attention to this aspect of his work. In doing so, we could better understand the development of not only specific fields (beside social anthropology, also other disciplines, such as archaeology, Old Testament studies, Biblical studies) during the last century, but also methodological approaches to the study of myths and rituals, as well as Smith's contribution to the study of comparative religion. His "interpretation of ritual in social terms" (as referred to by Rogerson 1979: 232) opened important insights for scholars from different disciplines—and remains still relevant today. There are some other aspects of his work, such as a discussion of ancient Babylonian and Phoenician creation stories—the third lecture of the third series of Smith's *Lectures on the Religion of the Semites* (Day 1995: 96–112)—which will strike readers as surprisingly contemporary. Smith's description of the cosmogony and analysis of the associated rituals in this case have withstood the test of time, and his analysis fits well with more recent research on this particular topic.

Smith's work was open to criticism (as he was well aware of—I noted instances when he would actually revise his views), and some of his ideas did not withstand the growth and development of subsequent scholarship. For example, Rogerson (1979: 232) writes, "If Robertson Smith made mistakes about nomadism, and used the comparative method backed by the doctrine of survivals, this was because like every one of us, he was a man of his own times. He was ahead of his times, however, in the way in which he sought to interpret religious data in sociological terms."

In lieu of a conclusion, I will quote Margit Warburg (1989: 56–57), who wrote of Smith:

His greatness is unanimously agreed upon . . . . This is remarkable, considering the fact that majority of the specific results of Robertson Smith's work on Semitic religion soon proved to be untenable. . . .

. . . what has caused Robertson Smith's greatness is not the validity of his theories, because most of the time he erred. It is possible, though, to err on several levels of creative originality. Robertson Smith's significance shows itself in the fact that his errors ruptured established frames and led to new insight.

Smith's complicated personal history, marked by loss of family members and illness, but also an absolutely brilliant scholarly career (Smith could easily have become a physicist or a mathematician), is characteristic of an eventful intellectual and personal journey. Smith was a man who was accused of promoting (and, in a sense, enabling) Orientalism, but who believed that Arabic was the closest language to the one that God spoke; a man who was asked to resign his teaching position in Aberdeen in 1881, after which he became the editor of the epoch-shifting edition of the *Encyclopædia Britannica* in 1883, and then reader and later professor of Arabic at the University of Cambridge; a man whose friends were John Ferguson McLennan and James George Frazer, whose influence was acknowledged by Émile Durkheim, and who was praised by Mary Douglas. Smith was a man fascinated by antiquity, but at the same time a great believer in progress, modernization, and the power of scientific method. This makes him one of the important ancestors of contemporary anthropology.

NOTE

The epigraph is from Smith 2002: 439.

SELECTED WORKS BY WILLIAM ROBERTSON SMITH

●　　●　　●

1875. "Bible." *EB⁹* 3: 634–648.

1886. "Sacrifice." *EB⁹* 21: 132–138.

1892 (1881). *The Old Testament in the Jewish Church: A Course of Lectures on Biblical Criticism*. London: Adam and Charles Black.

1902 (1882). *The Prophets of Israel and Their Place in History to the Close of the Eighth Century B.C.* With introduction and additional notes by T. K. Cheyne. London: Adam and Charles Black.

1907 (1885). *Kinship and Marriage in Early Arabia*. New edition, with additional notes by the author and Ignaz Goldziher, Budapest. Edited by Stanley A. Cook. London: Adam and Charles Black.

1912a (1880). "Animal Worship and Animal Tribes among the Arabs and in the Old Testament." In Black and Chrystal, *Lectures & Essays of William Robertson Smith*, 455–483. Originally published in the *Journal of Philology*.

1912b (1880). "A Journey in the Hejâz." In Black and Chrystal, *Lectures & Essays of William Robertson Smith*, 484–597.

1914 (1894). *Lectures on the Religion of the Semites: First Series, The Fundamental Institutions*. New edition, revised throughout by the author. London: Adam and Charles Black. First edition published in 1889.

REFERENCES

• • •

ABBREVIATIONS

EB   *Encyclopædia Britannica* (superscript denotes the edition).
ER   *Encyclopedia of Religion* (Mircea Eliade, ed., New York, 1987).
ERE *Encyclopædia of Religion and Ethics* (James A. Hastings, ed., Edinburgh, 1908–1926).
EU   *Encyclopædia Universalis* (Paris, 1990).
JST *Journal of Scottish Thought* (Aberdeen, 2008).
LCL Loeb Classical Library.

ARCHIVES

Christ's College, Cambridge.
Cambridge University Library, correspondence and papers.
University of Aberdeen Library, student notebooks with pasted-in newscuttings relating to the trial before Aberdeen Free Church Presbytery.
University College London, letters to G. C. Robertson.

WEBSITE

https://william-robertson-smith.net/en/
The site offers valuable information, including biographical notes, links to some important works, as well as many details of Smith's life. It is bilingual (German and English). The site is owned by Astrid Hess.

PRINCIPAL BIOGRAPHIC REFERENCES

Black, John Sutherland. 1900. "Smith, William Robertson." *Dictionary of National Biography*. Vol. 53, pp. 160–162. London: Smith, Elder & Co.

Black, John Sutherland, and George Chrystal. 1912a. *The Life of William Robertson Smith*. London: Adam and Charles Black.

———, eds. 1912b. *Lectures & Essays of William Robertson Smith*. London: Adam and Charles Black.

Booth, Gordon K. 1999. *William Robertson Smith: The Scientific, Literary and Cultural Context from 1866 to 1881*. PhD thesis, University of Aberdeen.

Bryce, James. 1903. "William Robertson Smith." In James Bryce, *Studies in Contemporary Biography*, 311–326. London: Macmillan & Co.

Burkitt, F. C. 1894. "William Robertson Smith." *English Historical Review* 9(36): 684–689.

Hess, Astrid, ed. N.d. The William Robertson Smith Website. Accessed 17 April 2018. https://william-robertson-smith.net/en/index.

Maier, Bernhard. 2009. *William Robertson Smith: His Life, His Work and His Times*. Forschungen zum Alten Testament 67. Tübingen: Mohr Siebeck.

Nelson, Donald R. 1969. *The Life and Thought of William Robertson Smith, 1846–1894*. PhD diss., Department of Humanities, Michigan State University, East Lansing.

Peters, E. L. N.d. "Smith, William Robertson." In *International Encyclopedia of the Social Sciences. Encyclopedia.com*. Accessed 26 November 2017. http://www.encyclopedia.com/social-sciences/applied-and-social-sciences-magazines/smith-william-robertson.

Salmond, S. D. F. 1894. "Professor William Robertson Smith." *Expository Times* 5(8): 356–361.

Sefton, Henry R. 2004. "Smith, William Robertson (1846–1894)." In *Oxford Dictionary of National Biography*. Oxford: Oxford University Press. Accessed 17 Feb 2017. http://www.oxforddnb.com/view/article/25939.

GENERAL REFERENCES

Ackerman, Robert. 1973. "Frazer on Myth and Ritual." *Journal of the History of Ideas* 34: 115–134.

———. 1987. *J. G. Frazer: His Life and Work*. Cambridge: Cambridge University Press.

———. 1991. *The Myth and Ritual School: J. G. Frazer and the Cambridge Ritualists*. New York: Garland Publishing.

———. 2001. "Jane Ellen Harrison: By Myth Begotten." *Religion* 31(1): 67–74.

———. 2007. "Cambridge Ritualists [Ritual Anthropologists]." *Oxford Dictionary of National Biography*. Accessed 19 June 2018. https://doi.org/10.1093/ref:odnb/95519.

———. 2008. "William Robertson Smith and J. G. Frazer: 'Genuit Frazerum'?" *JST* 1–2: 63–77.

———. 2015. "J. G. Frazer and Religion." In *BÉROSE, encyclopédie en ligne sur l'histoire des savoirs ethnographiques*. Paris: IIAC-LAHIC. Accessed 24 March 2019. https://www.berose.fr/article598.html.

Aeschylus. 1926. *Aeschylus*. With an English translation by Herbert Weir Smyth. Vol. 2. LCL. London: William Heinemann.

Ahlström, G. W. 1965. "Ivan Engnell (1906–1964)." *History of Religions* 4(2): 337–338.

Aijmer, Göran. 1987. "The Cultural Nature of Ritual and Myth." In Göran Aijmer, ed., *Symbolic Textures: Studies in Cultural Meaning*, 1–22. Gothenburg: Acta Universitatis Gothoburgensis.

Alcocer, Paulina. 2006. "La forme interne de la conscience mythique: Apport de Konrad Theodor Preuss à la Philosophie des formes symboliques de Ernst Cassirer." *L'Homme* 180(4): 139–170.

Alexander, H. B. 1924. "Worship (Primitive)." *ERE* 12: 752–757.

Amit, Vered, ed. 2004. *Biographical Dictionary of Social and Cultural Anthropology*. London: Routledge.

Anderson, G. W. 1950. "Some Aspects of the Uppsala School of the Old Testament Study." *Harvard Theological Review* 43(4): 239–256.

Anonymous. N.d. "William Robertson Smith & Religion of the Semites." Wordtrade.com. Accessed 27 May 2017. http://www.wordtrade.com/religion/bible/smithsemites.htm.

Ap-Thomas, D. R. 1966. "An Appreciation of Sigmund Mowinckel's Contribution to Biblical Studies." *Journal of Biblical Literature* 85(3): 315–325.

Bailey, Warner McReynolds. 1970. *Theology and Criticism in William Robertson Smith*. PhD diss., Yale University, New Haven.

———. 1973. "William Robertson Smith and American Bible Studies." *Journal of Presbyterian History* 51(3): 285–308.

Bediako, Gillian M. 1997. *Primal Religion and the Bible: William Robertson Smith and His Heritage*. The Library of Hebrew Bible / Old Testament Studies 246. Sheffield: Sheffield Academic Press.

Beidelman, Thomas O. 1974a. *W. Robertson Smith and the Sociological Study of Religion*. Chicago: University of Chicago Press.

———. 1974b. "Sir Edward Evan Evans-Pritchard (1902–1973): An Appreciation." *Anthropos* 69(3–4): 553–567.

———. 1987. "Smith, W. Robertson." *ER* 13: 366–367.

Benedict, Ruth. 1934. *Patterns of Culture*. New York: Houghton & Mifflin.

Blackman, A. M., C. J. Gadd, F. J. Hollis, S. H. Hooke, E. O. James, W. O. E. Oesterley, T. H. Robinson. 1933. *Myth and Ritual: Essays on the Myth and Ritual of the Hebrews in Relation to the Culture Pattern of the Ancient East*. Oxford: Oxford University Press.

Boas, Franz. 1888. "The Central Eskimo." In *Sixth Annual Report of the Bureau of American Ethnology*, 399–669. Washington, DC: Government Printing Office.

———. 1916. "Tsimshian Mythology, by Franz Boas, based on texts recorded by Henry W. Tate." In *Thirty-First Annual Report of the Bureau of American Ethnology to the Secretary of the Smithsonian Institution, 1909–1910*, 29–1037. Washington, DC: Government Printing Office.

Bolle, Kees W. 1987. "Myth: An Overview." *ER* 10: 261–273.

Boon, James A. 1987. "Anthropology, Ethnology, and Religion." *ER* 1: 308–316.

———. 2008. *Ethnographica Moralia: Experiments in Interpretive Anthropology*. New York: Fordham University Press.

Booth, Gordon K. 2002. "The Fruits of Sacrifice: Sigmund Freud and William Robertson Smith." *Expository Times* 113: 258–264.

———. 2009. "Comrades in Adversity: William Robertson Smith and Richard Burton." *Victorian Literature and Culture* 37(1): 275–284.

Borgeaud, Philippe. 1994. "Le couple sacré/profane: Genèse et fortune d'un concept 'opératoire' en histoire des religions." *Revue de l'histoire des religions* 211(4): 387–418.

Bošković, Aleksandar. 1988. "Razumeti mit" [To understand a myth]. *Polja* 355: 409–410.

———. 1989. "The Meaning of Maya Myths." *Anthropos* 84(1–3): 203–212.

———. 1992. "Great Goddesses of the Aztecs: Their Meaning and Functions." *Indiana* 12: 9–13.

———. 1995. "William Robertson Smith and the Anthropological Study of Myth." In Johnstone, *William Robertson Smith: Essays in Reassessment*, 303–310.

———. 2002. "Anthropological Perspectives on Myth." *Anuário Antropológico* 99: 103–144.

———. 2004. "Tylor, Sir Edward Burnett." In Vered Amit, ed., *Biographical Dictionary of Anthropology*, 523–525. London: Routledge.

————. 2006. *Mit politika ideologija. Ogledi iz komparativne antropologije* [Myth, politics, ideology: Essays in comparative anthropology]. Belgrade: Institute of Social Sciences.

————. 2010. *Kratak uvod u antropologiju* [A short introduction to anthropology]. Zagreb: Jesenski i Turk.

————. 2013. *"Legends of People, Myths of State. Violence, Intolerance, and Political Culture in Sri Lanka and Australia . . .* by Bruce Kapferer; *Contesting the State: The Dynamics of Resistance and Control* by Angela Hobart, Bruce Kapferer." Review. *Zeitschrift für Ethnologie* 138(2): 301–306.

————. 2017. *Mesoamerican Religions and Archaeology: Essays in Pre-Columbian Civilizations.* Oxford: Archaeopress.

Bošković, Aleksandar, Milan Vukomanović, and Zoran Jovanović, eds. 2015. *Rečnik božanstava i mitskih ličnosti sveta* [Dictionary of world deities and mythic personalities]. Belgrade: Službeni glasnik and Institute of Social Sciences.

Brown, Jesse H. 1964. *The Contribution of William Robertson Smith to Old Testament Scholarship, with Special Emphasis on Higher Criticism.* PhD diss., Graduate Program in Religion, Duke University, Durham, NC.

Burkert, Walter. 1980. "Griechische Mythologie und die Geistesgeschichte der Moderne." *Les Etudes classiques aux XIXe et XX siècles, Entrétiens sur l'antiquité classique* 26: 159–199.

————. 1985. *Greek Religion.* Translated by John Raffan. Cambridge, MA: Harvard University Press.

Campbell, Joseph. 1959–1970. *The Masks of God.* 4 vols. Harmondsworth: Penguin.

————. 2004 (1949). *The Hero with a Thousand Faces.* Commemorative ed. Princeton: Princeton University Press.

Carswell, Donald. 1927. *Brother Scots.* London: Constable and Co.

Cassirer, Ernst. 1922. *Der Begriffsform im mythischen Denken.* Studien der Bibliothek Warburg 1. Hamburg.

————. 1942. The Influence of Language upon the Development of Scientific Thought." *Journal of Philosophy* 39: 309–327.

————. 1944. *An Essay on Man: An Introduction to a Philosophy of Human Culture.* New Haven: Yale University Press.

————. 1946a. "Structuralism in Modern Linguistics." *Word* 1: 99–120.

————. 1946b. *The Myth of the State.* New Haven, CT: Yale University Press.

————. 1953 (1925). *Language and Myth.* Translated by Susanne K. Langer. New York: Dover Publications.

————. 1953–1957 (1923–1929). *Philosophy of Symbolic Forms.* 3 vols. Translated by Ralph Manheim. New Haven: Yale University Press.

Chantraine, Pierre. 1968–1980. *Dictionnaire étymologique de la langue grecque, histoire des mots.* 4 vols. Paris: Klincksieck.

Cohen, Percy S. 1969. "Theories of Myth." *Man,* n.s., 4(3): 337–353.

Cook, Stanley A. 1902. "Israel and Totemism." *Jewish Quarterly Review* 14: 413–448.

————. 1969 (1927). "Introduction" and "Additional Notes." In W. Robertson Smith, *Lectures on the Religion of the Semites: First Series, The Fundamental Institutions,* 3rd ed., Library of Biblical Studies. New York: KTAV Publishing House.

Craig, Cairns. 2008. "Editorial." *JST* 1–2: v–vii.

Darwin, Charles. 1968 (1859). *The Origin of Species by Means of Natural Selection, or the Preservation of Favoured Races in the Struggle for Life.* Harmondsworth: Penguin.

————. 1871. *The Descent of Man, and Selection in Relation to Sex.* London: J. Murray.

Day, John, ed. 1995. *The Religion of the Semites: Lectures on the Religion of the Semites (Second and Third Series) by William Robertson Smith.* Journal for the Study of the Old Testament Supplement Series 183. Sheffield: Sheffield Academic Press.

Detienne, Marcel. 1990. "Épistémologie des mythes." *EU* 15: 1048–1053.

Dominguez, Victoria R. 2018. "Lewis Henry Morgan, the Social Life of Invocations, and Me." In K. M. Mitrović and J. Ćuković, eds., *Društvo, nauka, progres [Society, science, progress]: Lewis Henry Morgan (1818–1881),* Conference Proceedings, 8–13. Belgrade: Department of Ethnology and Anthropology, Faculty of Philosophy.

Douglas, Mary. 1966. *Purity and Danger: An Analysis of Concepts of Pollution and Taboo.* London: Routledge and Kegan Paul.

————. 1995. "Demonology in William Robertson Smith's Theory of Religious Belief." In Johnstone, *William Robertson Smith: Essays in Reassessment,* 274–292.

Dresch, Paul. 1988. "Segmentation: Its Roots in Arabia and Its Flowering Elsewhere." *Cultural Anthropology* 3(1): 50 67.

Durkheim, Émile. 1968 (1912). *Elementary Forms of Religious Life.* Translated by Joseph Ward Swain. New York: Free Press.

Eliade, Mircea. 1959. *The Sacred and the Profane: The Nature of Religion.* Translated by W. R. Trask. New York: Harcourt Brace Jovanovich.

————. 1974 (1949). *Patterns in Comparative Religion.* Translated by Rosemary Sheed. New York: Meridian.

————, ed. 1987. *Encyclopedia of Religion.* 16 vols. New York: Macmillan.

Engnell, Ivan. 1967. *Studies in Divine Kingship in the Ancient Near East.* 2nd ed. Oxford: Basil Blackwell.

———. 1998. "New Year Festivals." In R. Segal, ed., *The Myth and Ritual Theory,* 136–140. Oxford: Blackwell.

Fallaize, E. N. 1924. "Prayer (Introductory and Primitive)." *ERE* 10: 154–158.

Feyerabend, Paul. 1981. *Problems of Empiricism.* Philosophical Papers 2. Cambridge: Cambridge University Press.

———. 1987. *Farewell to Reason.* London: Verso.

Fontenrose, Joseph. 1966. *The Ritual Theory of Myth.* Folklore Studies 18. Berkeley: University of California Press.

Frazer, James G. 1996 (1922). *The Golden Bough.* Abridged ed., with an introduction by George W. Stocking, Jr. Harmondsworth: Penguin.

Freud, Sigmund. 2001 (1913). *Totem and Taboo: Some Points of Agreement between the Mental Lives of Savages and Neurotics.* Authorized translation by James Strachey. London: Routledge.

Galinier, Jacques. 2004. "A Lévi-Straussian Controversy Revisited: The Implicit Mythology of Rituals in a Mesoamerican Context." *Journal of the Southwest* 46(4): 661–677.

Gaster, Theodor H. 1954. "Myth and Story." *Numen* 1(3): 184–212.

———. 1998. "Thespis." In R. Segal, ed., *The Myth and Ritual Theory,* 307–312. Oxford: Blackwell.

Geertz, Clifford, ed. 1971. *Myth, Symbol and Culture.* New York: W. W. Norton.

Glover, Willis B. 1954. *Evangelical Nonconformists and Higher Criticism in the Nineteenth Century Scotland.* London: Independent Press.

Goody, Jack. 1968. The Myth of a State. *Journal of Modern African Studies* 6(4): 461–473.

Gosden, Chris. 1999. *Anthropology & Archaeology: A Changing Relationship.* London: Routledge.

Greimas, A. J. 1971 (1966). "Elementos para uma Teoria da Interpretação da Narrativa Mítica." In Maria Zélia Barbosa Pinto, ed., *Análise Estrutural da Narrativa, seleção de ensaios da revista "Communications,"* 59–108. Petropolis: Editora Vozes.

Harrison, Jane Ellen. 1912. *Themis: A Study of the Social Origin of Greek Religion.* Cambridge: Cambridge University Press.

Harrelson, Walter. 1987. "Myth and Ritual School." *ER* 10: 282–285.

Herodotus. 1972. *The Histories.* Translated by Aubrey de Sélincourt. Revised, with an introduction and notes by A. R. Burn. Harmondsworth: Penguin Books.

Hocart, A. M. 1936. "Myth and Ritual." *Man* 36: 230.

Holdsworh, Chris. 2006. "Tylor, Sir Edward Burnett." *Oxford Dictionary of National Biography*. Accessed 9 April 2018. https://doi.org/10.1093/ref:odnb/36602.

Holloway, Steven W. 2000. "Review of *Lectures on the Religion of the Semites: Second and Third Series* by William Robertson Smith and John Day." *Journal of Near Eastern Studies* 59 (2): 137–140.

Holý, Ladislav. 1996. *Anthropological Perspectives on Kinship*. London: Pluto Press.

Homer. 1919. *The Odyssey*. With an English translation by A. T. Murray. 2 vols. LCL. London: William Heinemann.

———. 1924–1925. *The Iliad*. With an English translation by A. T. Murray. 2 vols. LCL. London: William Heinemann.

Hooke, S. H., ed. 1935. *The Labyrinth: Further Studies in the Relation between Myth and Ritual in the Ancient World*. London: Society for Promoting Christian Knowledge.

Houtman, Cornelius. 2000. Abraham Kuenen and William Robertson Smith: Their Correspondence. *Nederlands archief voor kerkgeschiedenis / Dutch Review of Church History* 80(2): 221–240.

Hvidtfeldt, Arild. 1958. *Teotl and *Ixiptlatli: Some Central Conceptions in Ancient Mexican Religion with a General Introduction on Cult and Myth*. Copenhagen: Munksgaard.

Hyman, Stanley Edgar. 1955. "The Ritual View of Myth and the Mythic." *Journal of American Folklore* 68(270): 462–472.

Ingold, Tim. 2004. "Anthropology at Aberdeen." *Aberdeen University Review* 60(211): 183–197.

Isambert, François-A. 1976. "L'Élaboration de la notion de sacré dans l' 'école' durkheimienne." *Archives de sciences sociales des religions* 21(42): 35–56.

Jacobs, Joseph. 1890. "Recent Research in Comparative Religion." *Folklore* 1(3): 384–397.

Johnstone, William, ed. 1995. *William Robertson Smith: Essays in Reassessment*. Journal for the Study of Old Testament Supplement Series 189. Sheffield: Sheffield Academic Press.

Jones, Jack. 1980. "Freud's Moses and Monotheism Revisited." *Ethics* 90(4): 512–526.

Jones, Robert Alun. 1984. "Robertson Smith and James Frazer on Religion: Two Traditions in British Social Anthropology." In George W. Stocking, Jr., ed., *Functionalism Historicized: Essays on British Social Anthropology*, 31–58. Madison: University of Wisconsin Press.

———. 1986. "Durkheim, Frazer, and Smith: The Role of Analogies and Exemplars in the Development of Durkheim's Sociology of Religion." *American Journal of Sociology* 92(3): 596–627.

———. 2005. *The Secret of the Totem: Religion and Society from McLennan to Freud*. New York: Columbia University Press.

Kapferer, Bruce. 1988. *Legends of People, Myths of State: Violence, Intolerance, and Political Culture in Sri Lanka and Australia*. Washington, DC: Smithsonian Institution Press.

Kaufmann, Yehzekel. 1951. "The Bible and Mythological Polytheism." *Journal of Biblical Literature* 70(3): 179–197.

Kirk, G. S. 1974. *The Nature of Greek Myths*. Harmondsworth: Penguin.

Kluckhohn, Clyde. 1942. "Myths and Rituals: A General Theory." *Harvard Theological Review* 35(1): 45–79.

Korotayev, Andrey. 1995. "Were There Any Truly Matrilineal Lineages in the Arabian Peninsula?" In *Proceedings of the Seminar for Arabian Studies*, vol. 25, 83–98. Oxford: Archaeopress.

Kraeling, E. G. 1928. "The Real Religion of Ancient Israel." *Journal of Biblical Literature* 47(1–2): 133–159.

Krois, John Michael. 1987. *Cassirer: Symbolic Forms and History*. New Haven: Yale University Press.

Kuper, Adam. 2016. "Anthropologists and the Bible: The Marett Lecture, April 2012." In Regna Darnell and Frederic W. Gleach, eds., *Local Knowledge, Global Stage*, 1–30. Histories of Anthropology Annual 10. Lincoln: University of Nebraska Press.

Lang, Andrew. 1884. "Mythology." *EB*⁹ 17: 135–158.

———. 1885. *Custom and Myth*. 2nd ed., revised. London: Longman's, Green, and Co.

———. 1887. *Myth, Ritual, and Religion*. 2 vols. London: Longman's, Green, and Co.

———. 1898. *The Making of Religion*. London: Longman's, Green and Co.

———. 1901. *Magic and Religion*. London: Longman's, Green and Co.

———. 1911. Mythology. *EB*¹¹ 19: 128–144.

Langer, Susanne K. 1971 (1942). *Philosophy in a New Key: A Study in the Symbolism of Reason, Rite, and Art*. Cambridge, MA: Harvard University Press.

Leach, Edmund R., ed. 1967. *The Structural Study of Myth and Totemism*. London: Tavistock Publications.

———. 1969. *Genesis as Myth and other Essays*. London: Jonathan Cape.

———. 1970 (1954). *Political Systems of Highland Burma: A Study of Kachin Social Structure*. London: Athlone Press, University of London.

———. 1985. "The Anthropology of Religion: British and French Schools." In N. Smart, J. Clayton, S. Katz, and P. Sherry, eds., *Nineteenth Century Religious Thought in the West*, vol. 3, 215–261. Cambridge: Cambridge University Press.

Leask, W. Keith. 1917. *Interamna Borealis: Being Memories and Portraits from an Old University Town between the Don and the Dee*. Aberdeen: Rosemount Press.

Levine, Baruch. 1997. "Review of *Lectures on the Religion of the Semites, Second and Third Series* [by William Robertson Smith] by John Day and William Robertson Smith." *Journal of the American Oriental Society* 117(3): 617.

Lévi-Strauss, Claude. 1958. "La Structure des mythes." In C. Lévi-Strauss, *Anthropologie Structurale*, 227–255. Paris: Plon.

———. 1963 (1958). "The Structural Study of Myth." In C. Lévi-Strauss, *Structural Anthropology*, 206–231. Translated by Claire Jacobson and Brooke Grundfest Schoepf. New York: Basic Books.

———. 1964–1971. *Mythologiques*. 4 vols. Paris: Plon.

———. 1978. *Myth and Meaning*. Toronto: University of Toronto Press.

———. 1987 (1984). *Anthropology and Myth: Lectures 1951–1982*. Translated by Roy Willis. Oxford: Basil Blackwell.

Lévy-Bruhl, Lucien. 1922. *La mentalité primitive*. Paris: Alcan.

Lewis, Herbert S. 2007. "The Influence of Edward Said and *Orientalism* on Anthropology, or: Can the Anthropologist Speak?" *Israel Affairs* 13(4): 774–785.

Linn, Will. 2018. "Joseph Campbell Is the Hidden Link between '2001,' 'Star Wars,' and 'Mad Max: Fury Road.'" *IndieWire*, 12 March 2018. Accessed 13 March 2018. http://www.indiewire.com/2018/03/joseph-campbell-heros-journey-2001-star-wars-1201937470/.

Livingstone, David N. 2004a. "Public Spectacle and Scientific Theory: William Robertson Smith and the Reading of Evolution in Victorian Scotland." *Studies in History and Philosophy of Science Part C: Studies in History and Philosophy of Biological and Biomedical Sciences* 35 (1):1–29.

———. 2004b. "Oriental Travel, Arabian Kinship, and Ritual Sacrifice: William Robertson Smith and the Fundamental Institutions." *Environment and Planning D: Society and Space* 22(5): 639–657.

———. 2015. "Finding Revelation in Anthropology: Alexander Winchell, William Robertson Smith and the Heretical Imperative. *BJHS* 48(3): 435–454.

Loyer, Emmanuelle. 2018. *Lévi-Strauss: A Biography*. Translated by Ninon Vinsonneau and Jonathan Magidoff. Cambridge: Polity Press.

MacDonell, Alice. 1933. "A Victorian Group." *The Deeside Field* 6: 35.

Malinowski, Bronislaw. 1926. *Myth in Primitive Psychology*. New York: W. W. Norton and Co.

———. 1961 (1922). *Argonauts of the Western Pacific*. New York: E. P. Dutton & Co.

Mandelbaum, David G. 1987. "Myths and Mythmaker: Some Anthropological Appraisals of the Mythological Studies of Lévi-Strauss." *Ethnology* 26(1): 31–36.

Maryanski, Alexandra. 2014. "The Birth of the Gods: Robertson Smith and Durkheim's Turn to Religion as the Basis of Social Integration." *Sociological Theory* 32(4): 352–376.

Masuzawa, Tomoko. 1989. "Original Lost: An Image of Myth and Ritual in the Age of Mechanical Reproduction." *Journal of Religion* 65(3): 307–325.

Maud, Ralph. 1989. "The Henry Tate–Franz Boas Collaboration on Tsimshian Mythology." *American Ethnologist* 16(1): 158–162.

Mauss, Marcel. 1950. *Sociologie et anthropologie*. 2 vols. Paris : Presses Universitaires de France.

McKinnon, Andrew. 2014. "Elementary Forms of the Metaphorical Life: Tropes at Work in Durkheim's Theory of the Religious." *Journal of Classical Sociology* 14(2): 203–221.

McLennan, John Ferguson. 1865. *Primitive Marriage: An Inquiry into the Origin of the Form of Capture in Marriage Ceremonies*. Edinburgh: Adam & Charles Black.

———. 1868. "Totem." In *Chamber's Encyclopedia*, supplement, 753–754. London: Chambers.

———. 1869–1870. "The Worship of Animals and Plants." *Fortnightly Review*, n.s., 4:407–427, 562–582; 7: 194–216.

Morgan, Kathryn. 2003. *Myth and Philosophy from the Presocratics to Plato*. Cambridge: Cambridge University Press.

Morgan, Lewis Henry. 1877. *Ancient Society or, Researches in The Line of Human Progress from Savagery through Barbarism to Civilization*. Chicago: Charles H. Kerr & Company.

Mowinckel, Sigmund. 1934. "'The Spirit' and the 'Word' in the Pre-Exilic Reforming Prophets." *Journal of Biblical Literature* 53(3): 199–227.

———. 1955. "Psalm Criticism between 1900 and 1935 (Ugarit and Psalm Exegesis)." *Vetus Testamentum* 5(1): 13–33.

Moyers, Bill. 2010. *Joseph Campbell and the Power of Myth with Bill Moyers*. Bonus Interview with George Lucas on mythology from *The Mythology of Star Wars*, conversation with Campbell from 1981 *Bill Moyers Journal*. Acorn Media/Athena.

Müller, [Friedrich] Max. 1909 (1856). *Comparative Mythology*. Edited, with additional notes and an introductory preface on solar mythology by A. Smythe Palmer. London: George Routledge and Sons.

Nash, Geoffrey, ed. 2009. *Travels to the Middle East from Burckhardt to Thesiger: An Anthology*. London: Anthem Press.

Nelson, Donald R. 1973. "The Theological Development of the Young William Robertson Smith." *Evangelical Quarterly* 45(2): 81–99.

Nöth, Winfried. 1990. *Handbook of Semiotics*. Bloomington: Indiana University Press.

O'Flaherty, Wendy Doniger, ed. and trans. 1975. *Hindu Myths*. Harmondsworth: Penguin.

———. 1988. *Other Peoples' Myths: The Cave of Echoes*. New York: Macmillan.

Overing, Joanna.1995. "O mito como história: Um problema de tempo, realidade e outras questões." *Mana* 1(1): 107–140.

Parman, Susan. 1995. "William Robertson Smith and American Anthropology: Science, Religion, and Interpretation." In Johnstone, *William Robertson Smith: Essays in Reassessment*, 264–271.

Partenie, Catalin. 2014. "Plato's Myths." In Edward N. Zalta, ed., *The Stanford Encyclopedia of Philosophy*, Summer 2014 ed. https://plato.stanford.edu/archives/sum2014/entries/plato-myths/.

Pindar. 1919. *The Odes of Pindar*. Including the principal fragments, with an introduction and an English translation by John Sandys. 2nd rev. ed. LCL 56. London: William Heinemann.

Plato. 1925. *Phaedrus*. In *Plato in Twelve Volumes*, vol. 9, translated by Harold N. Fowler. LCL 36. London: William Heinemann.

Pedersen, Esther Oluffa. 2008. "The Holy as an Epistemic Category and a Political Tool: Ernst Cassirer's and Rudolf Otto's Philosophies of Myth and Religion." *New German Critique* 104: 207–227.

Pedersen, Johannes. 1991 (1926/1940). *Israel: Its Life and Culture*. 2 vols. South Florida Studies in the History of Judaism 28. Atlanta: Scholars Press.

Peirano, Mariza, ed. 2001. *O Dito e o Feito: Ensaios de Antropologia dos Rituais*. Anthropology of Politics Collection. Rio de Janeiro: Relume Dumará.

Pfeffer, Georg. 2019. *Lewis Henry Morgan's Comparisons: Reassessing Terminology, Anarchy and Worldview in Indigenous Societies of America, Australia and Highland Middle India*. New York: Berghahn Books.

Popović, Aleksandar. 1987. "Reč i pojam Mythos" [The word and the concept of Mythos]. *Vidici* 251/252: 7–11.

Porter, J. R. 1977. "Two Presidents of the Folklore Society: S. H. Hooke and E. O. James." *Folklore* 88(2): 131–145.

Pritchard, James B, ed. 1991. *The Harper Concise Atlas of the Bible*. New York: Harper and Collins.

Propp, Vladimir. 1958 (1928). *Morphology of the Folktale*. Translated by Laurence Scott. International Journal of American Linguistics Series 24(4). Bloomington: Indiana University Research Center in Anthropology, Folklore, and Linguistics.

———. 1984. *Russkaia skazka*. Leningrad: University of Leningrad.

———. 1986. *Istoricčeskie korni volšebnoi skazki*. Leningrad: University of Leningrad.

Ptacek, Melissa. 2015. "Durkheim's Two Theories of Sacrifice: Ritual, Social Change and 'Les Formes élémentaires de la vie religieuse.'" *Durkheimian Studies / Études Durkhemiennes* 21: 75–95.

Radcliffe-Brown, Alfred Reginald. 1958. *Method in Social Anthropology: Selected Essays*. Edited by M. N. Srinivas. Chicago: University of Chicago Press.

Radin, Paul. 1957 (1937). *Primitive Religion: Its Nature and Origin*. New York: Dover Publications.

Ramnoux, Clemence. 1990. "Mythos et Logos." *EU* 15: 1039–1041.

Rapport, Nigel, and Joanna Overing. 2000. "Myth." In N. Rapport and J. Overing, *Social and Cultural Anthropology: The Key Concepts*, 269–283. London: Routledge.

Reinach, Salomon. 1911. "The Growth of Mythological Study." *Quarterly Review* 215: 423–441.

Ricœur, Paul. 1969 (1960). *The Symbolism of Evil*. Translated by Emerson Buchanan. Boston: Beacon Press.

———. 1987. "Myth and History." *ER* 10: 273–282.

———. 1990. "L'interprétation philosophique." *EU* 15: 1041–1048.

Rieff, Philip. 1954. "The Authority of the Past: Sickness and Society in Freud's Thought." *Social Research* 21(4): 527–550.

Riesen, Richard Allen. 1985. *Criticism and Faith in Late Victorian Scotland: A. B. Davidson, William Robertson Smith and George Adam Smith*. Boston: University Press of America.

Ringgren, Helmer. 1988. "Mowinckel and the Uppsala School." *Scandinavian Journal of the Old Testament Studies* 2(2): 36–41.

Rivière, Peter. 1995. "William Robertson Smith and John Ferguson McLennan: The Aberdeen Roots of British Social Anthropology." In Johnstone, *William Robertson Smith: Essays in Reassessment*, 293–302.

Rogerson, J. W. 1979. "Biblical Classics: IX. W. Robertson Smith: Religion of the Semites." *Expository Times* 90(8): 228–233.

———. 1995. *The Bible and Criticism in Victorian Britain: Profiles of F. D. Maurice and William Robertson Smith*. Journal for the Study of Old Testament Supplement Series 201. Sheffield: Sheffield Academic Press.

Rosati, Massimo. 2008. "Inhabiting No-Man's Land: Durkheim and Modernity." *Journal of Classical Sociology* 8(2): 233–261.

Rose, H. J. 1936. "Myth and Ritual." *Man* 36: 267.

Said, Edward W. 1995 (1978). *Orientalism: Western Conceptions of the Orient*. Harmondsworth: Penguin.

Saussure, Ferdinand de. 1985 (1916). *Cours de linguistique générale*. Edited by Tullio de Mauro; afterword by Louis-Jean Calvet. Paris: Payot.

Schmidt, Francis. 1994. "Des inepties tolérables. La raison des rites de John Spencer (1685) à W. Robertson Smith (1889)." *Archives de sciences sociales des religions* 39(85): 121–136.

Sefton, Henry R. 2007. "Religious Publishing." In D. Finkelstein and A. MacCleery, eds., *The Edinburgh History of the Book in Scotland*, 298–310. Edinburgh: Edinburgh University Press.

Segal, Robert A. 1980a. The Myth-Ritualist Theory of Religion. *Journal for the Scientific Study of Religion* 19: 173–185.

———. 1980b. In Defense of Mythology: The History of Modern Theories of Myth. *Annals of Scholarship* 1: 3–49.

———. 1992. "Joseph Campbell on Jews and Judaism." *Religion* 22 (2): 151–170.

———. 1997. *Joseph Campbell: An Introduction*. New York: Meridian.

———, ed. 1998. *The Myth and Ritual Theory: An Anthology*. Oxford: Blackwell.

———. 1999. *Theorizing about Myth*. Amherst: University of Massachusetts Press.

———. 2000. "Making the Myth-Ritualist Theory Scientific." *Religion* 30(3): 259–271.

———. 2001. "In Defense of the Comparative Method." *Numen* 48(3): 339–373.

———. 2008a. "William Robertson Smith vis-à-vis Émile Durkheim as Sociologist of Religion." *JST* 1–2: 1–12.

———. 2008b. "William Robertson Smith: Sociologist or Theologian?" *Religion* 38(1): 9–24.

———. 2011. "In Defence of Theories of Myth." *Cosmos* 26: 1–22.

———. 2015a. *Myth: A Very Short Introduction*. 2nd ed. Oxford: Oxford University Press.

———. 2015b. "Myth in Religion." In *International Encyclopedia of Social Sciences*, vol. 12, 172–178. Amsterdam: Elsevier.

———. 2017. "Theorizing Myth and Ritual." In Stefan Brink and Lisa Collinson, eds., *Theorizing Old Norse Myth*, 9–31. Acta Scandinavica 7. Turnhout: Brepols.

Settembrini, Marco. 2015. "William Robertson Smith e il suo *The Religion of the Semites* nelloro contesto storico-ideologico." *MeTeo* 8(1): 9–32.

Sharpe, Eric J. 1985. *Comparative Religion: A History*. 2nd ed. La Salle, IL: Open Court.

Silverstone, Roger. 1976. "Ernst Cassirer and Claude Lévi-Strauss: Two Approaches to the Study of Myth." *Archives des Sciences Sociales des Religions* 21: 25–36.

Skinner, Jonathan. 1994. "William Robertson Smith Congress." *Anthropology Today* 10(3): 21–22.

———. 1995. "Orientalists and Orientalisms. Robertson Smith and Edward W. Said." In Johnstone, *William Robertson Smith: Essays in Reassessment*, 376–382.

Smith, William Robertson. 1875. "Bible." *EB*[9] 3: 634–648.

———.1886. "Sacrifice." *EB*[9] 21: 132–138.

———.1892 (1881). *The Old Testament in the Jewish Church: A Course of Lectures on Biblical Criticism*. London: Adam and Charles Black.

———.1902 (1882). *The Prophets of Israel and Their Place in History to the Close of the Eighth Century B.C.* With introduction and additional notes by T. K. Cheyne. London: Adam and Charles Black.

———.1907 (1885). *Kinship and Marriage in Early Arabia*. New edition, with additional notes by the author and Ignaz Goldziher, Budapest. Edited by Stanley A. Cook. London: Adam and Charles Black.

———.1912a (1880). "Animal Worship and Animal Tribes among the Arabs and in the Old Testament." In Black and Chrystal, *Lectures & Essays of William Robertson Smith*, 455–483.

———.1912b (1880). "A Journey in the Hejâz." In Black and Chrystal, *Lectures & Essays of William Robertson Smith*, 484–597.

———.1914 (1894). *Lectures on the Religion of the Semites: First Series, The Fundamental Institutions*. New edition, revised throughout by the author. London: Adam and Charles Black.

———.1969 (1927). *Lectures on the Religion of the Semites: First Series, The Fundamental Institutions*. 3rd ed., with an introduction and additional notes by Stanley A. Cook. Prolegomenon by James Muilenberg. Library of Biblical Studies. New York: KTAV Publishing House.

———. 2002 (1894). *Religion of the Semites*. With a new introduction by Robert A. Segal. New Brunswick, NJ: Transaction Publishers.

Sophocles. 1919. *Sophocles*. With an English translation by F. Storr. Vol. 2. LCL 21. London: William Heinemann.

Sœbø, Magne. 1998. *On the Way to Canon: Creative Tradition History in the Old Testament*. Journal for the Study of Old Testament Supplement Series 191. Sheffield: Sheffield Academic Press.

Taylor, Bayard, ed. 1892. *Travels in Arabia*. Revised by Thomas Stevens. New York: Charles Scribner's Sons.

Thiele Smith, Alice. 2004. *Children of the Manse: Growing Up in Victorian Aberdeenshire*. Edited by Gordon K. Booth and Astrid Hess. Edinburgh: Bellfield Press.

Thomas, Bertram. 1929. "Among Some Unknown Tribes of South Arabia." *Journal of the Royal Anthropological Institute of Great Britain and Ireland* 59: 97–111.

———. 1932. "Anthropological Observations in South Arabia." *Journal of the Royal Anthropological Institute of Great Britain and Ireland* 62: 83–103.

Tylor, Edward B. 1871. *Primitive Culture: Researches into the Development of Mythology, Philosophy, Religion, Language, Art and Custom*. 2 vols. London: J. Murray.

Urban, Greg. 1991. *A Discourse-Centered Approach to Culture: Native South American Myths and Rituals*. Austin: University of Texas Press.

Verene, Donald Phillip. 1966. "Cassirer's View of Myth and Symbol." *The Monist* 50(4): 553–564.

———. 2015. *Vico's "New Science": A Philosophical Commentary*. Ithaca, NY: Cornell University Press.

Veyne, Paul. 1988 (1983). *Did the Greeks Believe in Their Myths?* Translated by Paula Wissing. Chicago: University of Chicago Press.

Vico, Giambattista. 1982 (1744). *Načela nove znanosti: o zajedničkoj prirodi nacija* [The principles of the new science: On the common nature of the nations]. Translated by Tatjana Vujasinović-Roić and Sanja Roić. Filozofska biblioteka. Zagreb: Naprijed.

Viveiros de Castro, Eduardo. 1992. *From the Enemy's Point of View: Humanity and Divinity in an Amazonian Society*. Chicago: University of Chicago Press.

Von Humboldt, Wilhelm. 1988 (1836). *On Language: The Diversity of Human Language-Structure and Its Influence on the Mental Develop-*

ment of Mankind. Translated by Peter Heath, with an introduction by Hans Aarsleff. Cambridge: Cambridge University Press.

Wach, Joachim. 1951. *Types of Religious Experience: Christian and Non-Christian*. Chicago: University of Chicago Press.

Warburg, Margit. 1989. "William Robertson Smith and the Study of Religion." *Religion* 19: 41–61.

Weitzman, Steven. 1997. "Revisiting Myth and Ritual in Early Judaism." *Dead Sea Discoveries* 4(1): 21–54.

Wheeler-Barclay, Marjorie. 1993. "Victorian Evangelicalism and the Sociology of Religion: The Career of William Robertson Smith." *Journal of the History of Ideas* 54(1): 59–78.

Widengren, Geo. 1945. "Evolutionism and the Problem of the Origin of Religion." *Ethnos* 10(2–3): 57–96.

———. 1957. "King and Covenant." *Journal of Semitic Studies* 2(1): 1–32.

———. 1971. "La méthode comparative: Entre philologie et phenomenologie." *Numen* 18(3): 161–172.

Wellhausen, Julius. 1899 (1883). *Prolegomena zur Geschichte Israels*. 5th ed. Berlin: Georg Reimer Verlag.

———. 1973 (1885). *Prolegomena to the History of Ancient Israel*. Translated by J. Sutherland Black and Allan Menzies; preface by William Robertson Smith. New York: Peter Lang.

Yamani, Mai. 2009 (2004). *Cradle of Islam: The Hijaz and the Quest for Identity in Saudi Arabia*. London: I. B. Tauris.

Young, Michael. 2004. *Malinowski: Odyssey of an Anthropologist, 1884–1920*. New Haven: Yale University Press.

INDEX

● ● ●